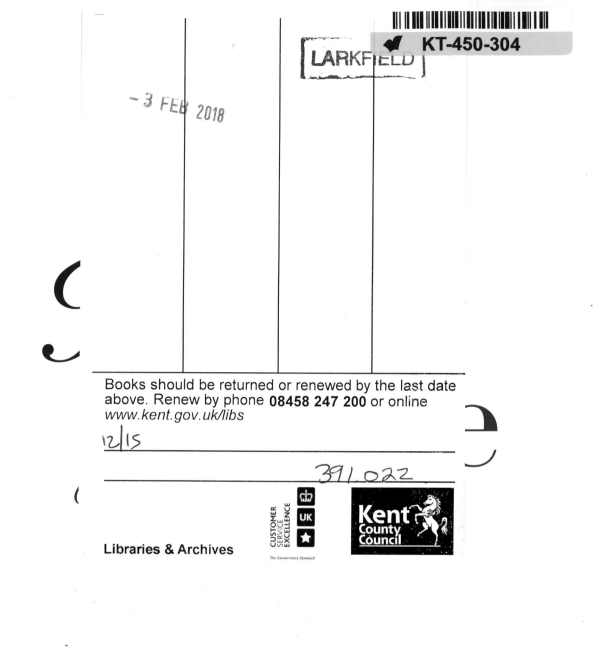

Kate Style

Chic and Classic Look

Alisande Healy Orme

Plexus, London

Contents

Chapter 1

From School to Sloane

'Kate was very much the prettiest girl on campus. '

Contemporary at the University of St Andrews

Catherine Elizabeth Middleton was born to Carole and Michael Middleton on 9 January 1982. Kate's first home was in the village of Bradfield Southend in Berkshire, one of the Home Counties that surround London. Her parents had a comfortable, semi-detached red brick Victorian house, tucked away down a quiet lane.

In 1987, Carole Middleton set up Party Pieces, a company that provided ready-made goody bags for children's parties. By 1995 the business was booming and the family moved into a much larger house in the nearby village of Bucklebury. Although it only takes an hour to reach London, the pretty village, with its wholesome sense of community, seems worlds away from the grit of the city.

Growing up in the Home Counties was undoubtedly one of the earliest influences on Kate Middleton's sense of style. It's a running joke in Britain that nice girls from those areas can be picked out a mile away, so different is their dress sense from that of their urban contemporaries. Their top priority being to look nice and elegant, the country girls' style exists in a kind of bubble, untouched by the latest fashion trends.

In 2010 celebrity hairdresser Nicky Clarke said of Kate, '[She] has had a typical, non-offensive look that has never been too scary, but not much to shout about either. It's a simple, shire girl kind of look,' which rather sums up the look but misses the point. Home Counties girls make a calculated decision to look 'non-offensive'; it is their first step towards not only being classy, but also classic dressers. Their style may not change or develop much beyond their late teens, but that is because, like Kate Middleton, they tend to find the looks that suit them, and stick with them.

School Days: St Andrew's and Downe House

In 1986, at the age of four, Kate started Bradfield Church of England Primary School, which was next door to the family home. By 1989, however, Party Pieces was already proving such a success that the Middletons made the decision to move their eldest daughter to the exclusive St Andrew's Preparatory School, a private school four miles away. 'Back then,' says Kingsley Glover, a former classmate, 'Kate was completely different – shy, skinny.'

Kate updates traditional tweed with a statement belt and Spanish riding boots at the Game Fair at Blenheim Palace in 2004.

Kate at St Andrew's Prep School, where she was known for her hard work and determination.

❛ Catherine Middleton was a bright, popular and extremely capable pupil.
I am delighted for her and the whole college joins me in wishing
her and Prince William great happiness together. ❜

Nicholas Sampson, Master of Marlborough College, 16 November 2010

In spite of always being reserved, Kate is also remembered for her good looks which, like her temperament, were already apparent. 'She was one of the most beautiful girls in the year, and made such an impression that she became something of a legend in local public schools when we moved on,' said one former classmate.

At the age of thirteen, Kate moved to Downe House; an all-girls' boarding school in Berkshire, where she was apparently bullied for being 'pale, quiet [and] shy'. Only a year later – and halfway through the academic term – the concerned Middletons pulled their daughter out of the school, sending her instead to one of the country's top public schools, Marlborough College, where gangly, shy Kate would begin to blossom into the elegant young woman we see today.

Initially homesick, once Kate had settled into school life she became known as a hard worker who did well academically and excelled at sport. It was not until the age of sixteen, returning to school after the summer holidays, that she really began to be noticed for her looks. According to Gemma Williamson, who also attended Marlborough, '[The September after GCSEs] Catherine came back an absolute beauty. She always had a lovely, willowy figure, but now she had filled out and the colour was back in her cheeks. Although she was sporty, she was very feminine, too. She never wore particularly fashionable clothes – just jeans and jumpers – but she had an innate sense of style.'

Marlborough College

6 Famous, designer label, co-ed boarding school still riding high. 9

The Good Schools Guide

Founded in 1843 on the outskirts of an attractive market town in the county of Wiltshire, Marlborough College is one of Britain's leading boarding schools. In 1969 the school became the first major English public school to introduce girls at sixth form, becoming fully co-educational in 1989. The school is known for its academic excellence, as well as its reputation for sports, which is bound to have appealed to the naturally athletic Kate.

Along with conventional sports such as hockey, netball and lacrosse, girls can enjoy extracurricular activities such as shooting (the school has its own range), polo horse riding, and skiing – pursuits that have undoubtedly helped Kate to fit in with her future in-laws, who are well known for their love of the outdoors and country sports.

Other Old Marlburians include Kate's future cousin-in-law Princess Eugenie, children's author and illustrator Lauren Child, songwriters Chris de Burgh and the late Nick Drake, and artist and writer William Morris.

In Her Trunk: What Kate is Likely to Have Packed for School

Uniform

Marlborough requires girls to don a bright turquoise tartan kilt worn below the knee over navy-blue tights or knee-high socks, a white v-neck blouse, a navy blue v-neck jumper, and blue college blazer. These clothes are often worn oversized.

Older girls are allowed to exchange their kilt for a black skirt, which, according to school uniform regulations, 'must graze the floor'. These are still worn with the white blouse and navy jumper. Marlborough tend to encourage a more refined approach to grooming. In other words, the girls' hair is worn down, mostly in flattering tousled styles such as the one Kate still favours.

In sixth form, girls may wear mufti (army slang-derived, boarding-school speak for a student's own clothes) as long as it fits in with certain guidelines, which are mostly geared towards making sure they look smart. For example, no denim skirts or jeans can be worn to lessons.

❛ Days [at Marlborough] were spent sweeping through the grounds dressed in our uniform: a floor-length black skirt that harked back to the Victorian era. ❜

Clarissa Sebag-Montefiore, former Marlborough pupil and classmate of Pippa Middleton

Flat shoes

It is compulsory for female students to wear flat black shoes with their school uniform.

Sports kit

A keen sportswoman, who apparently excelled at rounders, hockey and netball, it's doubtful that Kate ever forgot her trainers, gym skirt or sweatshirt – all embroidered with the school crest. Like any other little Marlburian preparing for school, Kate would have bought her kit from Crosby and Lawrence. Located near the school, Marlborough bought out 'Cros and Los' fifty years ago and they have been supplying the school exclusively ever since.

Mufti

In boarding schools, where students are constantly surrounded by their peers, their home clothes, or mufti, take on a special importance. There is not only the usual teenage pressure to 'fit in', but also pressure to comply with a certain way of presenting oneself that hints at students' social status. Kate would have felt this,

Left and centre: Crisp white blouses and knitted sweaters have been Kate's wardrobe staples since her school days.
Right: Training with her 'sisters' for a twenty-one-mile, cross-channel boat race in 2007. Kate's love of sport began at school.

and there are hints of it in her personal style today, when the backbone of her wardrobe could have come straight out of her packing trunk.

Bootcut jeans

A staple of nineties dressing, these are flattering on the leg, and can be teamed with blouses rather than t-shirts, for a smart-casual look. Photos of Kate from her Marlborough days show that she favoured this look outside of school hours, and she still does. Kate picks up her classic blue bootcuts at Crew Clothing.

T-shirts and blouses

Multiple, in both v- and round-neck. Even at that age, Kate was a fan of the smart-casual look that has stood her in such good stead, so these are likely to have come from quality high-street shops such as Reiss and her future employer, Jigsaw.

Ralph Lauren Cable Knit Jumpers

Perfect for staying cosy in draughty dormitories, and later hunting lodges.

Cardis

The cardigan, a girlier alternative to a jumper, has always suited Kate's innately feminine style. As an adult, she favours cashmere, but it's likely that the ones she wore at school were plain old lambswool. Again, Jigsaw and their sister company Kew are good bets for these.

Fleeces and Barbour jackets

More practical than cute, these decidedly sensible items are nonetheless often found in the wardrobes of boarders, especially those who, like Kate, enjoy country pursuits.

A 'good' coat and tailored jackets

If there is one item Kate Middleton has always known her way around, it is a beautifully tailored coat, preferably to the knee. She also wore tailored jackets to school, proving that her eye for style was already developing.

Maxi skirts

Which could have been worn to church and classes.

A suit for church

A necessary part of the uniform list at a school where attending church on Sundays was essential. This may have been when Kate first realised that tailoring really suited her.

Boots

Did Kate's boot obsession first begin at school? She would certainly have worn them under jeans, with skirts, and with her church suit.

Heels

Along with her smart boots, Kate may well have kept a pair of black court shoes on standby for formal events.

University of St Andrews

❛When I first met Kate I knew there was something very special about her. ❜

Prince William on their first meeting as students at St Andrews in 2001

After leaving Marlborough, Kate took a gap year. She spent part of it in Florence, where she studied art, taking in the city's astonishingly beautiful frescoes, sculptures and the Basilica di Santa Maria del Fiore; the Duomo (or cathedral) for which the city is celebrated.

Later, she volunteered at a school in Chile. Her trip to the developing country was organised through Raleigh International, a youth and education programme that provides opportunities for people to take part in expeditions and charitable projects in South America, India and Indonesia. In a turn of events that romantics might deem fated, only six short months after Kate had finished volunteering and returned to the UK, Prince William would arrive in Chile to take part in the same programme. The couple were, it seems, meant to meet.

Raleigh International leader Rachel Humphreys, who looked after Kate and the other volunteers, remembers her as having 'a certain presence . . . She was a very mature girl, attractive and popular – particularly with the boys. But she was always in control of herself and impeccably behaved.' A few months later Kate enrolled at university where, after four years, she would graduate with a 2:1 degree and the love of a Prince.

Right and overleaf: Kate gains a Master of Arts degree from St Andrews University in 2005.

6 Before they met she'd already been voted the prettiest girl at St Salvator's Hall [where she and Wills were in halls]. 9

OK! *magazine, December 2010*

The St Andrews Look

St Andrews is notable as one of the few universities in the UK to still require its students to wear academic robes for all formal occasions, including pier walks, meetings of the Union Debating Society, attending chapel and sitting exams, something which, along with its isolated location and the climate in that part of the country, undoubtedly affects the dress of its students.

Hannah Betts of *The Daily Telegraph* has said that while '[at] St Andrews, Kate sported the Fulham-by-Sea, jeans Puffa and pashmina combo favoured by students to beat the haar, the local mist. Her own haar was not groomed, her look unstudied.' This low-key look helped her blend in with the rest of the small student population where 'everyone knows everyone', and which, according to *Vanity Fair* magazine, is known for its 'niceness'. Her understated style was probably also part of the reason that Prince William – a royal who has always shown himself to be a man of the people – fell for her.

Other photos of Kate during this time show that her personal style, though not as sleek as it would become by the time of her engagement, was already developing. A picture of her dancing with William at a university bop (as they are known at St Andrews) shows her wearing a black wrap dress, sheer black tights and black court shoes – three items that continue to be staples of her wardrobe today. Other girls at the party are wearing cocktail dresses in styles now condemned to the fashion graveyard. By sticking to her style guns in what may have seemed a less exciting choice at the time, Kate has achieved many women's dream: she looks timelessly stylish but still exactly like herself.

The Fashion Show: How Kate Met Her Match

Kate's see-through dress immediately became the stuff of tabloid legend, and rumours quickly circulated that the beautiful girl modelling it was in a relationship with Prince William; a piece of gossip that soon became the truth. Although the show was not the first time he had laid eyes on his future bride, it was apparently the first time he realised that he wanted to get to know her better. Ben Duncan, a friend of William's, revealed that when he saw Kate on the catwalk the Prince exclaimed,

'"Wow, she's hot!" His eyes were literally on stalks and came out of his head! She brushed by him on the way to the catwalk and things were never the same again – the whole history of the monarchy had been altered.'

Charlotte Todd, who designed the dress, speculates that 'maybe if it hadn't have been see-through, William might not have noticed her'. While this statement seems doubtful in light of the couple's long-term commitment to each other, not to mention Kate's good looks and their wealth of mutual friends, her now-legendary appearance in this dress is notable for being one of the few times Kate has dressed so racily. Well, it was for a good cause!

❢ It's a part of fashion history– the moment when William could first have fallen in love with Kate. ❢

Charlotte Todd, who designed the famous see-through dress that Kate modelled in a 2002 charity fashion show at St Andrews.

Left and opposite: Kate makes a lasting impression on a young Prince William at a university fashion show in 2005.

Chapter 2

The New Sloane Ranger

' There's no question that Sloanes seem more relevant again. It's partly cyclical, partly a reaction to the bland modernism of the past ten years and also to the jaw-dropping vulgarity. '

Peter York, author of The Official Sloane Ranger Handbook

The term 'Sloane Ranger' was coined by the writer Peter York in his 1982 book *The Official Sloane Ranger Handbook*. It refers to a certain type of Brit that many people assumed had died out after the 1980s – the socially-driven, upper-class young person who lived and hung out around Chelsea and the King's Road. Sloane women were always on the lookout for suitably wealthy and preferably titled husbands, while Sloane men liked to party alongside women of the same ilk. The book's cover featured stereotypical Sloane boys and 'gels', including a photograph of Sloane Ranger par excellence Princess Diana, who had lived in a Kensington flat bought for her by her father and, before becoming engaged to the Prince of Wales at the grand old age of nineteen, could usually be found on the King's Road. The Victorian look and sepia tint of the book's cover are suggestive of the traditionalist values of most Sloanes. The brilliant BBC2 documentary series *British Style Genius*, which aired in September 2008, said of first-generation Sloanes:

'The traditionalist views and behaviours of Sloanes included a predilection for the countryside and their wardrobe reflected this.

'Britain in the early 1980s was a perfect breeding ground for the Sloane style, with the connotations of money and the conservative attitude it entailed. Resolutely conformist, their look comprised a loyalty to what their parents and grandparents had worn. It was the perfect look for well-bred boys and girls from the country who wanted to show they were above fashion and a little bit posh.

'When the world started to learn about Lady Diana Spencer in 1981, it was the trigger that took the Sloane style into the mainstream. Diana wore traditional country clothes familiar to the upper classes, but made them visible nationally, becoming the archetypal Sloane Ranger.'

For many commentators, Kate Middleton – a well-connected girl from the countrified middle-classes who enjoys browsing in every Sloane's favourite department store Peter Jones – is proof that Sloane Rangers are alive and well.

> ❛Kate has been a Peter Jones customer for years and she's told us she'll continue to come here when she's married to William.❜
>
> *A saleswoman at the department store Peter Jones*

Kate looks breezy and stylish in a red polka-dot wrap dress at the Chakravarty Cup polo match in 2006.

A Brief History of Sloanes

	Then	Now
Who?	Lady Diana Spencer, later Princess Di. Sarah Ferguson, later the Duchess of York. TV style gurus Trinny and Susannah. (Susannah dated the Queen's nephew, Viscount Linley.) It-girl Tara Palmer-Tomkinson. Heiress Jemima Goldsmith, later Khan.	Kate Middleton, Princess-in-waiting. Pippa Middleton, Kate's sister. Chelsy Davy, Prince Harry's sometime squeeze. Henry Conway, party promoter, journalist and son of MP Derek Conway.
Defining Features	Links to the royal family, either through noble blood or a parent whose military career meant they worked for 'the firm'. Committed traditionalists, nationalists and monarchists.	Expert social networkers with aristocratic and probably royal connections. Today's Sloanes are less likely to be born into the nobility, but they probably went to school with them.
Where to Find Them?	In South-West London, though they'd have preferred to be in the country. Husband-hunting around King's Road, Kensington Square and Sloane Square. Living in family-owned flats in London SW3. Their trust funds mean they don't have careers, making them free to visit the country as often as they like. Also frequently sighted in the Royal Enclosure at Ascot, at the Chelsea Flower Show or possibly working a season as a chalet girl in Val d'Isere.	In *Tatler*'s party pages. Today's Sloanes are more likely to work than their predecessors, and so stay in London longer. They can be found partying at all the more exclusive nightclubs like Boujis and Mahiki (their Crack Baby cocktails are Kate's favourite). Working Sloanes favour jobs in the media. Ideally in PR and advertising, but they will settle for being 'in fashion'. Aged eighteen to twenty, Sloanes can be found pursuing gap years in parts of South America and Africa. They are also more likely to be found in higher education than their predecessors.
How to Spot Them?	Braying laughter. Decidedly dodgy hair. The non-ironic wearing of pussy-bow blouses.	Classic dressing bordering on conservative with a special emphasis on the use of prints. A grooming regime that includes glossy hair and manicures but still manages to appear thoroughly 'English' (meaning nothing showy).

Clockwise from top left: Original Sloane Ranger, Princess Diana; A frilly Lady Sarah Ferguson takes typical Sloane 'matchy-ness' to excess; Nouveau-Sloane Pippa Middleton in a chic wrap dress at the Guards polo club; Kate in a classically feminine summer ensemble.

Sloane Princesses

❛ Kate is much more fashion savvy than Diana was at the start.

She's more in control of herself. She knows how to work a look already. ❜

Peta Hunt, fashion director, You & Your Wedding

As far back as March 2007, Peter York admitted that the level of public interest in the new generation of high-profile Sloanes such as Kate Middleton and Prince Harry's on-off girlfriend Chelsy Davy had prompted him to begin revising *The Sloane Ranger Handbook*. When asked about the comparisons between his late former cover star Diana and her son's bride-to-be, York noted that, 'Being more of a middle-class Sloane than Diana, [Kate] is less flaky. We're not going to see her turn Euro-fabulous.'

Kate's background has all the hallmarks of a nouveau Sloane. She is boarding-school educated and attended St Andrews, a good university that a lot of other upper-class public-school types attend (other Sloane favourites: Bristol, Exeter, Edinburgh and Oxbridge). She achieved a thoroughly respectable 2:1 in her History of Art degree, but since then only appears to have worked when she has chosen to, hinting at her family's affluence. After graduating, she moved into a £1m flat that her parents bought for her on Chelsea's Old Church Street, but has never spent much time there as she's devoted much of the past five years to supporting Prince William's military career, meaning that she's frequently moved up and down the country.

Kate's own professional experience has been limited to a part-time job in fashion at Jigsaw and a stint working for her parents. She has been criticised by many for her perceived lack of professional ambition, accused like Princess Diana before her of being another trust-funded Sloane who planned to 'slum it' on the London scene until she found a husband.

Though their sense of style has developed in the years since Princess Diana first became famous, today's Sloanes have yet to shake their long-standing image as ambitionless 'It-girls'.

On her 25th birthday, Kate wears a monochrome print dress from high-street fashion chain Topshop; the dress famously sold out as soon as Kate was seen wearing it.

Career Moves

❛ [Kate has] been offered every job under the sun. Russian oligarchs, fashion designers – everyone wants her. But if she goes out and works, she'll be accused of abusing her connections – or of being used . . . What can she do? She's in a very difficult position. ❜

A Middleton family friend, Vanity Fair, *November 2008*

In the years between Kate's graduation and engagement, the British media concerned themselves with much more than her relationship with Prince William. Whatever she did, wherever she went, intense speculation followed. Her school life was reported on, as were her later career choices, or the perceived lack of them. Amongst the criticism levelled at 'work-shy Kate' were claims that even the Queen thought she should get a job.

Arguably, this criticism is unfair. At various points Kate has worked, although maintaining a typical nine-to-five existence has been made extremely difficult by paparazzi intrusion and Prince William's military obligations. At the time of her engagement she had been employed in a PR and marketing role at Party Pieces, her parents' mail-order company, for at least two and a half years. Her lawyer Gerald Tyrell also confirmed in 2008 that Kate had taken a graphic design course to enable her to design the company's catalogues and marketing materials.

It's easy to see why Kate may prefer working for her parents, who also employ her sister Pippa and brother James. Her previous job, in the (Sloane favourite) fashion industry, had unfortunately not been so low-profile.

In November 2006, Kate accepted a job as part-time accessories buyer for Jigsaw Junior, the children's department of high-street fashion chain Jigsaw, a company owned by John and Belle Robinson, who are acquaintances of her parents.

The role of accessories buyer involves sourcing items such as belts, bags, hats, headbands, shoes and jewellery that will be sold in stores across the country. While at Jigsaw, Kate collaborated on a necklace for teenage girls with jewellery designer Claudia Bradby, wife of ITV reporter Tom, who conducted the first interview with Kate and William upon the announcement of their engagement.

Kate looks every inch the sophisticated city girl in these stylish, workaday ensembles.

Of the simple necklace – a silver chain which had a large silver broad bean at the centre, with a smaller pink crystal bead on one side, and a pearlised caramel one on the other – Bradby said, 'Kate was very clear in what she wanted. She wanted a very simple bean pendant that a mother and daughter could both wear together. It was completely her initiative because she thought there was a gap in the market for something real and sophisticated, that had longevity for that age group.'

The delicate, understated necklace perfectly encapsulates Kate's style. Very much influenced by her own mother, Kate always goes for classic pieces, many of which are appropriate for both generations (she has even been known to lend accessories to her mother). In December 2010, Jigsaw confirmed that the necklace will be reissued at a cost of £46, to coincide with excitement about the royal wedding.

Carole Middleton (left) borrows her daughter's hat for Royal Ascot in 2010, and Kate (right) wears the same lavender-blue Philip Treacy hat to the wedding of Nicholas Van Cutsem in 2009.

Talking about Kate's role in the company, which lasted for one year, Belle Robinson said that Kate had contacted her personally and asked for a job with 'an element of flexibility to continue the relationship with a very high-profile man and a life she can't dictate . . . I have to say I was so impressed by her. There were days when there were TV crews at the end of the drive. We'd say, "Listen, do you want to go out the back way?" And she'd say, "To be honest, they're going to hound us until they've got the picture. So why don't I just go, get the picture done, and then they'll leave us alone."'

Now that Kate is about to embark on her new career as an integral part of the modern monarchy – including a key role in the Queen's Jubilee in 2012 – she must surely feel a certain sense of triumph for having survived the last decade of media scrutiny with no more scandal attached to her name than the nineteen-year-old Lady Diana Spencer. An achievement in the age of gossip magazines and twenty-four-hour media coverage.

> ❛ Kate and the chain's signature aesthetics match perfectly: she is the embodiment of the Sloane revival and wore Jigsaw clothes long before she started working for them. ❜
>
> The Guardian, *17 March 2007*

Get the Look:
The New Sloane Ranger

Sloanes favour what the French call 'classic dressing', which is often branded too conservative (read: too much like their mothers). The key is to hit on the kind of timeless outfit you could still be wearing in thirty years' time. Kate's tailored blazers from (her mum's favourite) Hobbs, or mid-heeled suede boots by Boden, while not the latest fashion fads, will never really go out of style because they are never going to be 'on-trend'. As Coco Chanel once said, 'Fashion comes and goes but style lasts forever.'

Carole and Kate Middleton shopping in Sloane Square department store Peter Jones.

Remember: it's not about looking cutting-edge; it's about looking nice – respectable, well-mannered and well-to-do. Classic print dresses and pastel-coloured cardis are as popular with today's Sloanes as they were when Diana was strutting her stuff on King's Road. Unlike past Sloanes, Kate's floral frocks are usually from high-street stores like Jigsaw and LK Bennett. Other city staples include black suede boots, bootcut jeans and maxi shopper bags. For every occasion glossy, swishy hair is a must.

Floral frocks, bootcut jeans and slouch boots are amongst Kate's favourite casual items.

Sloanes always keep a good supply of tweeds, knitwear and shooting gear on hand for days in the country. Boutique King's Road designer Katherine Hooker keeps Kate well-supplied with custom-made tweed coats and jackets for days at the races, while more active pursuits demand Hunter wellies and waxed Barbour jackets – but only in green.

Top-to-toe tweed: Kate puts a modern, feminine twist on a country staple.

Wear things your boyfriend and his friends will find non-threatening – Sloanes are nice girls, always decorous but always discreet. In the quest for love, marriage and the chicest wardrobe possible, Sloanes always look the part.

Kate looks cool and casual at summer sporting events. Left: A polo match at Englefield House. Right: Beaufort Polo Club.

Newly single Sloanes should go for all-out glamour. Short skirts, sequins, satin bib-front dresses in bright colours, even a bit of cleavage – it's all fair game if you've lost your man. During her break from William, Kate showed off an array of uncharacteristically skimpy party dresses, mostly from Topshop and French Connection, and reportedly won him back by attending a fancy dress party dressed as a 'naughty nurse'.

Kate hits the London club scene in a series of thigh-skimming party dresses during her break from William in 2007.

Chapter 3

Princess Style

❛ There is a classicism in her choices that **projects fashion** but not outrageously so. I think what's remarkable is that so early in the process she has found **an identity of her own** and that is something that will enhance her authenticity. This is someone we are going to be deeply compelled by for a long time to come. **❜**

Hamish Bowles, European editor, American Vogue

Once her engagement was announced, Kate's sense of style swiftly became a matter of public interest. Questions such as 'Where does she buy her clothes?' and 'How much does she spend on them?' were asked. Parts of her wardrobe – the Issa dresses, LK Bennett footwear, and Jigsaw skirts – were easy to identify, but others seemed to leave even seasoned fashion editors scratching their heads.

On 13 January 2011, *New York* magazine offered some insight into why it's so hard to find out where Kate's clothes are from when they reported – perhaps erroneously – that Kate's favourite shop is in fact every bargain hunter's first port of call, TK Maxx. TK Maxx is an American-owned chained of outlet shops (known in the US as TJ Maxx) that sells a huge range of designer bags and clothing for up to sixty percent off their original price. A source told the magazine that, '[Kate] loves to shop for bargains, mixing and matching high-street clothes and designer. She has a great eye for that.'

The very next day *The Daily Telegraph* contributed to the solving of Kate's fashion conundrum. In an article entitled 'Thrifty Kate Middleton Causes Designer Headache', the following was reported:

'Each time the fiancée of Prince William is pictured in a new outfit, many of which she has bought in the sales, fashion houses are deluged with interest.

'"It's a nightmare because our archives don't go back that far," whines one fashionista. "I wish she would start wearing from the current season as it's almost impossible to confirm anything when the items are so old."'

It is amusing to think that Kate's thriftiness and habit of recycling her favourite items of clothing many times over – which most people would surely consider admirable, especially in light of Britain's current economic climate – has sent ripples of panic throughout fashion houses.

Kate Middleton's sense of style has been compared to all manner of well-dressed women, from American First Ladies such as Michelle Obama and Jackie Kennedy to Carla Bruni, the elegant former supermodel who married the French President Nicolas Sarkozy in 2008, and wowed the British press with the purple and grey wardrobe she donned for an official visit to the UK that same year. Kate has even been compared with the woman who would have been her mother-in-law, the late Princess of Wales.

When she is married Kate will begin a life of royal duty that will see her thrust

Kate sparkled in metallic grey at the Time to Reflect *book launch party in 2007.*

‘ I love her style confidence! In the US, we have a recessionista in the White House in Michelle Obama, who shops at the Gap, J. Crew, Talbot's, H&M and other retailers. Now it looks like a recessionista may just step into the palace . . . although Kate's style may change when she becomes Princess of Wales, as did Diana's. Stay tuned as the evolution of style continues. ’

Mary Hall, The Huffington Post,
16 December 2010

Kate shows off her stunning figure in a sleek and sexy white lace dress arriving at the 2007 launch of Simon Sebag Montefiore's book, Young Stalin.

into the public eye, putting her sense of style under even greater scrutiny. Certain fashion magazines have suggested that she should, as Diana did, call upon the help of a professional stylist. Diana relied on Anna Harvey, who was then deputy editor of British *Vogue*, but it seems that Kate, who has had occasional help from Leesa Whisker's style consultancy and personal shopping service, the Whisker Agency, will continue to dress well, should she choose to employ a personal stylist or not.

Whisker's services, though similar, should not be confused with those of a personal stylist: the Whisker Agency determines how a person wants to look and then helps them shop for appropriate clothing. A personal stylist, on the other hand, is employed to completely reinvent their client's image.

A famous recent example of this kind of reinvention might be hotel heiress Paris Hilton's transformation (around the time of her 2006 arrest for driving under the influence) from a trashy 'celebutante' – whose wardrobe consisted mainly of hot pants, tacky mini dresses, velour tracksuits, and a myriad of false hair pieces – to a 'respectable businesswoman', who wore blazers, matching separates, pearls, and neatly styled hair that was often pulled up into a bun. This kind of makeover, plainly made to convince a judge and jury of Hilton's respectability, is one Kate is never likely to need. Should she employ a stylist it's more likely that, like Princess Diana, she will use them to inject glamour into her wardrobe.

But, as of right now, Kate seems to embody legendary *Vogue* editor Diana Vreeland's fashion maxim that: 'The only real elegance is in the mind; if you've got that the rest really comes from it.' It's to be hoped that she'll be able to retain an elegance that seems to be very much innate, in spite of the inevitable pressure of public life and her high-profile marriage.

The actress Carey Mulligan, herself a fashion 'It-girl', known for a sophisticated sense of style that has never hinged on provocative or revealing clothing, has said that, '[Kate] never looks like she's trying to be anyone else and she's comfortable in her own skin.' It's already known that Prince William is trying to 'learn from past mistakes' when it comes to Kate's introduction to life in the royal family; there are even rumours that she's been sent to counselling to help her cope with the stress and upheaval involved.

It's also rumoured that the Countess of Wessex, formerly Sophie Rhys-Jones, has offered to act as an advisor to Kate. Sophie, another middle-class girl who married into the royal family after her eight-year courtship of William's uncle Prince Edward, is said to be the only one of her children's spouses with whom the Queen has had a consistently good relationship, making her an ideal candidate to advise Kate on potentially tricky issues such as etiquette and the minutiae of royal life.

Kate, a Princess who came from the people and won them over by dressing and behaving like the nice middle-class girl she is, is now lauded as a style icon the world over. Alexa Chung, another nice middle-class girl who has achieved style icon status over the past few years, had this to say about her: 'I think she's pretty, elegant and classy, and graceful – all the things that someone in the royal family should be.'

❛ Kate is beautiful and elegant. For the royals, apparently the royal blood is not in demand any longer [which will be] better for the generation to come . . . She is very different from Princess Diana, and seems a very well-balanced and a happy person. She is chic in a way the position needs. ❜

Karl Lagerfeld, New York *magazine, 18 November 2010*

Dressing to Impress: Kate's Wardrobe Staples

Dresses

Wrap dresses

Diane von Furstenberg, who invented wrap dresses, has said that 'the wrap dress was an interesting cultural phenomenon, and one that has lasted thirty years'.

In the first photograph of Kate and William that indicated they might be a couple, Kate was wearing a wrap dress, and has continued to wear Issa, Fenn Wright Manson, Diane von Furstenberg, and even Topshop versions of the dresses ever since, often in a print to flatter her already enviable figure.

Single-colour dresses

Kate's collection of single-colour dresses, in fabrics including silk jersey, tends to make itself known at more formal events such as the announcement of her engagement, the weddings of her friends, and evening events.

She usually chooses a full-length maxi style in a plain colour for formal evening events, but sticks to knee-length for daytime events such as weddings. Her preference for plain, single shades at more formal events marks out her sophistication. She has the height to carry off maxi dresses, and is slender enough to render them elegant, rather than frumpy.

Issa has for a long time acted as 'old faithful' when it comes to Kate's evening wear, though she has also worn a stunning turquoise dress by BCBGMAXAZRIA, and was recently spotted buying a few pieces by Aussie designer Collette Dinnigan. If she plays her cards right Dinnigan – a designer favoured by Prince William's cousin Princess Eugenie – may just find herself in the enviable position of being Kate's favourite member of the commonwealth.

> ‘A girl should be two things:
>
> # classy and fabulous.’
>
> *Coco Chanel*

Kate looks stunning in single-colour, silk jersey maxi dresses by her favourite designer Issa.

Print and patterned day dresses

Kate's preferred dresses come in a jersey fabric and often feature a print of some sort, although floral slip dresses worn under a cashmere cardi are Kate's outfit of choice when the weather starts to warm up. For example, she owns both the black and white versions of the 'Lucky' summer dress by Issa. (Hollywood A-listers Hilary Swank and Scarlett Johansson, and *Sex and the City* star Kristin Davis have also been spotted in the dress.)

Kate looks fresh and summery in two versions of the short, but sweet 'Lucky' dress by Issa.

Out and about in London. Whether teaming her skirts with boots, wedges or flats, Kate always keeps her hemlines above the knee to show off her perfect legs.

Skirts

Kate has been spotted in both maxi and pencil skirts, but has recently begun to favour A-line shapes that fall to the knee and flare out. Though she is never really casual, skirts do contribute towards her most casual looks. As such, these tend to come from high-street shops such as Jigsaw, Reiss and Whistles.

Because she is blessed with slim hips, a tiny waist, and long shapely legs, Kate can pretty much wear any style of skirt she chooses. Her habit of accessorising them with either flat knee boots or wedge-heeled shoes not only makes both items more flattering – even on great legs – but is also an effective way to make an otherwise dressy outfit smart-casual. Careful use of appropriate accessories really is the key to this look.

Jeans

Though her height and build would allow her to pull off any style she wants, Kate is often seen in what many women consider their 'safety jeans' – the kind of blue bootcuts or slightly flared styles that are always flattering, and go with virtually anything.

Kate's are usually from the American high-street brand J. Crew or designer label 7 For All Mankind. She usually teams them with boots – which she wears both over and under them – or her wedges (never trainers), camisole tops, and smart tailored jackets to create her trademark smart-casual look.

She also has a penchant for white jeans à la Liz Hurley, which she wears in the summer with blouses, Breton tops and her favourite wedge heels.

Hats and Fascinators

No woman in the public eye wears hats with quite as much aplomb as Kate Middleton; her hat collection is both fabulous and classy, and almost exclusively made up of pieces from the world's greatest living milliner, Galway-born Philip Treacy. Kate attends a lot of weddings and race days, for which she needs formal hats or fascinators. She loves to wear them casually too, and has been known to pitch up in everything from knitted berets to corduroy trilbies for everyday use. The kinds of hats that suit you depend very much on your face shape. Oval faces such as Kate's can pull off virtually any variety of headwear, as their even proportions do not need to be balanced out by any particular style.

Footwear

Knee-high boots
Usually in suede with a low or medium heel. 'Regulation Middleton uniform,' according to *Sunday Times Style* magazine, these can be – and have been – worn everywhere, and come from good quality brands such as Kurt Geiger, LK Bennett, and Boden.

Wedge shoes
With a medium heel and open toe, wedges are the perfect choice of footwear for polo matches. The flat sole is perfect for stomping down the divots, while the medium height gives just enough life to make the outfit more smart than casual. Kate's are from KG at Kurt Geiger, and she also likes to team them with jeans, camis and blazers for daytime in the city, and print dresses for when she hits the London club scene.

Court shoes
Preferably in suede or satin and almost always from LK Bennett, with the odd interruption from Kurt Geiger for more casual styles. Court shoes are Kate's staple for formal events. Most often in black, she has recently started to experiment with other colours such as navy blue and a warm pink nude.

Whether at the polo (left) or out in the city (centre, right), jeans are one of Kate's favourite casual choices.

Jewellery

Her engagement ring

By Garrards, obviously. For reasons that aren't so much superstitious as potentially embarrassing, Kate is unlikely to ever be seen without her ring. Should a paparazzo take a snap of her bare left hand, rumours would swiftly fly around the globe that her marriage was in trouble – something to be avoided.

Dangly earrings

Kate's favourite items of jewellery. Before she became engaged, earrings were often the only jewellery she wore. Since then, she has begun to favour matching necklace and earring sets in shades that compliment her outfits. These have tended to come from Links of London, but the odds are on William investing in some higher-end pieces for her from jewellers such as Asprey over the next few years.

Long necklaces

Now and again Kate has been known to accessorise a casual outfit with a pendant that hangs on a long chain, including a blue quartz heart pendant on a length of suede, which she wore over a jumper in a similar shade. The Lola Rose necklace was bought for Kate by William for the modest sum of £45 and will be reissued this year.

Bracelets

As with all her jewellery, Kate tends to go for delicate, understated bracelets, like the simple gold chain she frequently wears on special occasions. In 2009, she wore a Swarovski Daisy Chain bracelet to compliment a grey Issa maxi dress at an event for Starlight, a children's charitable foundation that her parents are involved with. Kate has also been known to sport a 'Power Balance bracelet', which the press were quick to poke fun at. The silicone band contains a hologram, which is said to banish negativity from the body and improve health and fitness. Although many celebrities, including sportsmen and Hollywood A-listers, have been spotted wearing the bands, their Australian manufacturer admits there is no proof that they actually work.

Right: Showing off her athletic figure in a floaty summer dress, teamed with a little black belt and practical espadrille wedges at the Chakravarty Cup polo match in 2010, and (far right) Kate works the cowgirl look at the Gatcombe Horse Trials in 2005.

Tailoring

Kate is blessed with a stunning figure that apparently had modelling agencies clamouring to sign her up while she was still at university. Never a sexy dresser, she uses tailored jackets and coats that nip in at the waist to show it off in a classy – rather than racy – way. Her favourite fitted blouses achieve the same effect. Kate buys her staple fitted jackets from high-street stores like Fenn Wright Manson, Hobbs, Jigsaw and LK Bennett. She also has an enviable collection of pieces from London boutique designer Katherine Hooker, who, in what must be a masterpiece of Sloane marketing, also designs matching pashminas.

Trench Coats

A trench coat is the perfect bridge between classic, smart tailoring and sexy, grown-up clothing. According to Hilary Alexander, fashion editor of *The Daily Telegraph*, Kate wore a 'white-hot trench coat from the red-hot label, Issa' to the Wembley concert for Princess Diana in 2007. She also wore a full-skirted navy trench that was rumoured to be from Burberry Prorsum, accessorised with a trilby and black knee-high boots, to the 2008 Cheltenham races.

Cardigans

Though her style veers more towards smart than casual, Kate has been known to substitute a cardigan for her usual tailored jacket or coat, particularly as the weather grows warmer. Her favourites have come from high-street shops such as J. Crew and Jigsaw, though she also has a soft spot for BCBGMAXAZRIA's tie-front belted style in heather-grey, which shows off her tiny waist.

Other Tops

Kate is occasionally seen in a jumper, which she layers over t-shirts and under jackets to give a preppy, rather than scruffy, look. These come from brands such as Ralph Lauren, for cable knits, and Boden for plain knits.

Kate looks her classic best for a day at the races in a full-skirted navy trench coat and trilby.

Get the Look

City Girl

Jackets, jeans and fitted blouses, worn with boots in winter and peep-toe wedge heels in summer. Also for summer: slip dresses worn with cardis, and those same wedge shoes. Do not forget your earrings. As for accessories, Kate likes a big handbag – all the better to hide any purchases from paparazzi lenses. She usually opts for Longchamp handbags in neutral shades but has also been spotted with an uncharacteristically flashy Mulberry Araline bag in fuchsia.

Country Girl

Waxed jackets, fleeces, jeans, and wellington or hacking boots for shoots or stalking weekends. These can be exchanged for tweedy-looking Katherine Hooker suits and coats worn with a striking hat or fascinator if you are attending either the Cheltenham Festival or the races. Chanel sunglasses may be used to shield your eyes from the sun.

Evening Formal

A long, preferably silk maxi dress in a single bright colour such as red, pink or turquoise. Evening dresses can be worn with court shoes, and feel free to adopt longer, sparklier earrings than you'd usually wear. Evening weddings require a fascinator in a colour that matches your dress.

Evening Casual

Not necessarily casual as you know it. This is an opportunity to don your best printed wrap dress, pull on your suede knee boots or wedges, and hit the dance floor. Again, always accessorise with a really good pair of earrings.

Wedding Guest Chic

Choose a colour palette and stick to it, be it blue and black, red and black, pink and black, cream on cream, or blue on blue. The clothes you choose should flatter your body, and show it off whilst still allowing you to appear demure. Your best bet is always a dress, worn with a smart tailored jacket or coat, and accessorised with court shoes, a box clutch bag and a little something by Philip Treacy on your head.

Fancy Dress

If possible, it's best not to be photographed in this, in order to avoid being embarrassed in the tabloids. That said, if there's an opportunity to dress up, embrace it. Roller-skating disco vixen, naughty nurse, and sparkly vampire are all outfits that Kate has worn.

Clockwise from top left: Perfectly co-ordinated Kate matches her blouse and bag for a smart city look; A refined tweed ensemble at the Cheltenham Horse Racing Festival, May 2007; Looking sleek and stylish at the Boodles Boxing Ball in 2008; Showing off tanned and toned legs in day-glo fancy dress and her favourite black suede boots at a charity roller disco in 2008; Simply stunning in an electric blue dress, black fitted blazer and picture hat at a friend's wedding in 2010; Oozing sophistication in a black and gold silk dress with bangles and a shrug to match at a 2006 birthday party in Chelsea.

Chapter 4

Wedding Guest Style

' Prince William's girlfriend is a great hat-wearer … I have designed for her and she is beautiful, so hats will go on. '

Milliner Philip Treacy on Kate Middleton's ongoing love affair with headwear

'She has an elegant, refined style which is modern and fresh.'

Bruce Oldfield

Before her engagement, Kate's status as a reluctant public figure meant that she had never given an interview. For the most part, the public perception of her hinged on two factors: what she did in her social life, and what she wore while doing it.

It's probably telling that the future Princess, whose own wedding has been yearly predicted by the media, never looks better than on other people's wedding days. Her understated grooming, defiantly grown-up clothing, and especially her love of hats and fascinators really come into their own on days devoted to joining couples in Holy Matrimony. And, though she always dresses smartly, Kate's day-to-day wardrobe largely consists of pieces that have been carefully chosen from shops at the upper end of the high street. Weddings mark the few occasions when she splashes out on designer clothing, giving her the opportunity to truly shine

Kate's apparent fascination with fascinators and other varieties of headwear (particularly those by celebrity and society favourite milliner Philip Treacy) is enough to make one wonder why Kate didn't train as a milliner herself. It's hard to think of another woman in the public eye who wears hats quite so frequently, and so well.

Significantly, when she made *Vanity Fair*'s International Best Dressed List in 2008 it was, 'Because,' the magazine explained, 'we're throwing her hats in the ring.'

Kate and William attend the wedding of Harry Meade and Rosemarie Bradford shortly before the announcement of their own engagement.

Kate's Best Wedding Outfits

The Marriage of Rose Astor and Hugh Van Cutsem, June 2005

Kate wore: A beige and black outfit that won her Most Promising Newcomer in *The Daily Telegraph*'s 2006 style awards. A short fitted jacket, possibly from Hobbs, over a horizontal striped pencil skirt made from panels of black and white lace, teamed with a small black straw fascinator worn on the side of her head, and black LK Bennett court shoes.

The Marriage of Laura Parker-Bowles and Harry Lopes, May 2006

Kate wore: A chic brocade dress coat in cream that she likely had made especially for the wedding of William's step-sister, a significant and possibly quite intimidating event to be invited to. She teamed the subtle statement piece with beige court shoes, and a striking brown and beige two-tone feather fascinator by Philip Treacy.

The Marriage of Autumn Kelly and Peter Phillips, May 2008

Kate wore: A short pink fitted jacket with a low v-neck and eighteenth-century-style double row of buttons over a black chiffon dress that flared to the knee and had a sheer panel over the décolleté. The striking jacket is likely to have been bought off the peg, possibly from Fenn Wright Manson. To finish the outfit she chose pink silk LK Bennett court shoes that perfectly matched her blazer, and a black straw pill-box hat by – who else? – Philip Treacy. Though the ensemble was criticised by some for being 'too matchy', she would later wear the hat, jacket and shoes again, albeit as parts of other outfits.

Right: Kate wears a beige and black ensemble to the Oxford wedding of Hugh Van Cutsem and Rose Astor in 2005 and (far right) 'A great hat wearer': Kate makes a statement in a dramatic feather fascinator by Treacy at the wedding of Laura Parker-Bowles in 2006.

The Marriage of Lady Rose Windsor and George Gilman, July 2008

Kate wore: A floaty chiffon print dress in shades of blue under a well-fitted, pale-blue short jacket – both were perfect for a wedding held at the height of summer. The jacket is believed to be from Fenn Wright Manson, while the dress could well be Whistles. Her accessories were black suede court shoes, a blue and black patterned Temperley clutch, and a black feather fascinator by Philip Treacy. She avoided a wardrobe malfunction by wearing a flesh-coloured slip under her frock, so that when the wind flipped her skirt, her legs were not revealed.

The Marriage of Chiara Hunt and Rupert Evetts, September 2008

Kate wore: A bright yellow fitted blazer over a black and yellow floral print skirt, and no notable accessories, or hat. Photographs from the event make it hard to pick out the details of the outfit, but safe to say, it's not one of her most memorable ensembles.

The Marriage of Alice Hadden-Paton and Nicholas Van Cutsem, August 2009

Kate wore: A bluebell-coloured brocade coat that she apparently had made for her by Edinburgh graduate Jane Troughton, who has also dressed Laura Bailey and Jodie Kidd. Fitted at the waist, it reached the knee and was worn over a knee-length pale grey chiffon dress, with midnight-blue satin LK Bennett court shoes, and accessorised with a blue snakeskin Jimmy Choo box clutch. A Philip Treacy fascinator in a matching shade of blue topped off the outfit. The light blue disc perfectly matched the paler shades in the pattern of Kate's dress coat, while the rose attached below the crown mirrored its darker parts. In June 2010, her mother Carole would be spotted wearing this fascinator at Ascot.

Right: Kate perfects her summer look in the blue chiffon print dress she wore to Lady Rose Windsor and George Gilman's July 2008 wedding, and (far right) the bluebell brocade coat she had custom-made for Alice Hadden-Paton and Nicholas Van Cutsem's August 2009 nuptials.

The Marriage of Emilia d'Erlanger and David Jardine-Paterson, April 2010

Kate wore: Red! A genuine splash of colour in the form of this bright red dress by Issa – the same designer who made her blue engagement dress – at the wedding of one of her closest friends from school and university. She teamed the bat-winged dress, which also had a sexy open back, with a pair of large sparkly earrings made of interlinking circles, and a bright red Philip Treacy fascinator made of a red silk flower with matching netting.

The Marriage of Lucy Regan and Charlie Savory, May 2010

Kate wore: A very pretty outfit in a neutral shade. The same eighteenth-century-style fitted jacket and pale pink shoes she wore to Peter Phillips's wedding, this time teamed with a white lace pencil dress, possibly from Whistles, and clutch bag in a complimentary colour. Rather than a fascinator or hat, Kate pulled the top section of her hair back from her face using a pale pink rose clip. This hairstyle was unusual for Kate as she usually wears her hair fully down for public events.

Kate was a vision in red at the April 2010 wedding of Emilia d'Erlanger and David Jardine-Paterson (left), while (right) an eighteenth-century influence is visible in the pale fitted jacked she chose for Lucy Regan and Charlie Savory's May 2010 marriage.

The Marriage of Melissa Nicholson and Oliver Baker, May 2010

Kate wore: The same beige brocade coat she wore to Laura Parker-Bowles's wedding four years earlier. She teamed it with black patent LK Bennett court shoes, sheer black tights, and the black pillbox hat previously worn to Peter Phillips's wedding.

The Marriage of Rosemarie Bradford and Harry Meade, October 2010

Kate wore: A cobalt blue Issa dress, with an A-line skirt that flared to the knee, a short tailored black jacket that showed off her tiny waist, and pointy black LK Bennett court shoes. Her other accessories included a small black box clutch by Temperley, and understated gold jewellery. Her Philip Treacy chapeau was reminiscent of those Christian Dior designed for the 'New Look' collection in 1947; a large black straw disc, adorned with a few large feathers on the crown, worn at a jaunty angle.

The Marriage of Sarah Louise Stourton and Harry Aubrey-Fletcher, January 2011

Kate Wore: Black. Defying the cold weather and the convention that dictates one should not wear black to a wedding, Kate chose the same dress she had donned at the wedding of Autumn Kelly and Peter Phillips. An eye-catching black chiffon piece, with a floaty A-line skirt and semi-sheer bodice, the dress had previously been covered with a modesty-preserving blazer, rather than the more revealing black velvet dress coat with diamante clasp Kate chose for this event. The silk velvet 'Dulwich' coat was by Libélula, the brand owned by former Temperley designer Sophie Cranston. Kate finished the dramatic outfit with a black pillbox hat by English hat manufacturers Whitely Fischer, purple suede shoes with a bow detail, and a matching clutch bag.

Right: Kate wore this tailored beige brocade coat to two weddings; first in 2006, and again in 2010, while (far right) she triumphantly defied the convention that one shouldn't wear black to a wedding in the daring chiffon piece she chose for Sarah Louise Stourton and Harry Aubrey-Fletcher's January 2010 marriage.

Chapter 5

Hair and Beauty

6 Kate [has] the ultra-slender figure 21st-century celebrity culture demands, and on a good day that blow-dried chestnut mane and golden skin tone can give the other national sweetheart, Cheryl Cole, a run for her money. 9

Jess Cartner-Morley, The Guardian, *17 November 2010*

❛ Our relationship with the Middletons has been built on discretion and trust . . . our stylist, James Pryce, did a fantastic job in enhancing Kate's look for the engagement press day. ❜

Richard and Hellen Ward

In November 2010 Mary Greenwell, the legendary make-up artist who was responsible for transforming Princess Diana from a girl-next-door into a diva, told *The Daily Telegraph* that she was '. . . so happy William met Kate when she was slightly puppy-fatty and beautiful [because] she's certainly become more of a lady in the past few months. There's no huge difference in her make-up, but it's more polished.'

What Greenwell meant, and it's a sentiment that has been repeatedly echoed throughout the media in relation to women and their jobs, is that now she looks better, Kate is a far better candidate. To look the part is to be it, which is why, however politically incorrect it may be, Kate Middleton's appearance is important.

Whether Kate's weight loss and improved grooming is due to the pressure of being in the public eye, or simply part of growing up, the way she looks has changed in the past few years: she's thinner and more toned, her hair is straighter, bouncier and glossier, her skin more radiant, her make-up more polished, and her nails manicured.

Though she is rarely given much credit for her public image, Kate has been clever about it, making these subtle changes look like a natural evolution rather than a big effort. Yet, as beautiful and uncalculated as she looks, her sophistication has been interpreted negatively, and Kate has found herself described as a modern-day Stepford wife or WAG.

Hannah Betts, a feminist journalist and one of Kate's fiercest critics, said in *The Daily Telegraph* that when she got engaged, 'Miss Middleton – lofty-haired and resplendent in blue – resembled a Sloane Cheryl Cole, as if she had landed a L'Oréal contract rather than a royal engagement.'

But despite such ungallant criticism, Kate has successfully transformed herself from fresh-faced schoolgirl to modern beauty icon. Style.com, the online home of American *Vogue*, even presented her as its beauty icon of the month in June 2008, proving that, as far as everyone who's not Hannah Betts is concerned, she's certainly making the beauty grade.

Fascinators such as this delicate feathery black piece are a favourite accessory of Kate's when dressing for society weddings.

Hair: From Natural Beauty to Glossy Goddess

The televised announcement of Prince William and Kate Middleton's impending nuptials brought three things into sharp focus: the ring, the dress, and her hair. So enviably bouncy and glossy were Kate's locks that day that *Heat* magazine suggested she might have employed hair extensions, stating, 'Either she's taking more than one bottle into the shower or that's the best goddamn weave we've ever seen.'

Celebrity hairdresser Nicky Clarke might feel that until she got engaged, 'Kate [always] had a typical, non-offensive look that has never been too scary, but not much to shout about either . . .' but even at school and university – before she'd discovered the benefits of a professional blow-dry and still wore her hair in loose natural waves – the length and condition of Kate's chestnut locks made her stand out in a crowd mostly made up of other nicely groomed ex-public schoolgirls.

Kate graduated from St Andrews in 2005, quickly moving into a flat her parents had bought for her in Chelsea, a part of London that in the minds of the English will forever be Sloaney. With the move came increased attention from paparazzi, and this renewed interest in her life and appearance, along with her new non-student status, might be why – in late 2005 – Kate began visiting stylist James Price at celebrity hairdresser Richard Ward's Salon and Metrospa.

The so-called 'Super Salon', a two-minute drive from Kate's flat on Old Church Street, offers beauty treatments such as fake tanning, facials, hair removal, massages, manicures and pedicures, as well as all kinds of hair treatments. Coincidentally, it is based just off Sloane Square, the stomping ground of one Lady Diana Spencer before her wedding to Prince Charles. Kate, along with other posh clientele such as Tara Palmer-Tomkinson and Lady Isabella Hervey, visits Richard Ward every five or six weeks for a cut and infusion blow dry that costs a relatively modest £105 per visit. According to the salon, the 'Infusion Blow Dry's revolutionary technology allows us to speed dry and condition in one step. Using the heat of the generated air to infuse the active ingredients deep into the hair shaft, it delivers stunning and instant results.'

Much to the disappointment of women across the country, James Price has remained tight-lipped about which products he uses to create the volume and shine of Kate's hair. Many beauty writers agree that, though it would be time-consuming, with practice it is possible to recreate Kate's engagement hair-do at home.

Right: A beautifully-groomed Kate leaves her hairstylist. Far right: Kate wore this elegant feathered disc hat to St George's Chapel in Windsor for the 2008 ceremony during which Prince William was officially made a Knight of the Garter.

Get the Look:
Very Much a Hair-Do

Kate's Engagement Hairstyle

- Start by washing your hair using a volumising shampoo and conditioner. Richard Ward's Salon and Metrospa sells Couture Hair, Ward's own brand of shampoo and conditioners, through their website. Chances are that James Price is using Couture Hair VoluMoist shampoo and conditioner to keep Kate's locks well-conditioned, as well as bouncy.

- Kate probably also uses the Couture Hair Clay Mineral Masque and Silk Protein Masque intensive conditioning treatments to keep her hair looking healthy in between trips to the salon.

- After washing, apply a root life product all the way from the roots to the ends of your hair. Couture Hair make a Volumiser Root Booster spray that 'leaves you with lustrous, volumous hair with hold, but without residue or stickiness'. Although there are other, less costly products on the market that can achieve similar results.

- Blow-dry your hair so it's eighty percent dry, then divide it into sections.

- Take a medium-sized round bristle brush, and roll a section of hair around it. Holding the brush away from your head (exposing about two to three centimetres of roots), start blow-drying on a medium heat with the hairdryer pointing down the shaft of the hair. It is essential to make sure that your hair is totally dry before moving onto the next section.

- The natural bristles will help to create a natural shine in the hair, while pulling the brush away from the head will help create even more volume.

- Once you have finished blow-drying all your hair, take a few large Velcro rollers and set them in the top section of your hair in a forward-facing direction. Once they are in place blast them with cold air and leave them to set.

- Remove the rollers. The front section of your hair should fall naturally, giving soft movement.

- Spritz your locks with a light-hold hair spray and you're good to go!

At the official public announcement of Kate and William's engagement, Kate's shiny, full-bodied hairstyle created almost as many headlines as the engagement itself.

Skin Care and Make-Up

The Swiss Method

In November 2010 it was confirmed that Kate uses Swiss skin-care brand Karin Herzog to keep her skin looking healthy and glowing. Founded by Dr Paul Herzog, a Noble Prize honouree, the company pioneered the use of oxygen in beauty products. According to Julie Cichocki, Kate was introduced to the brand by a friend and 'uses the Professional Cleanser (£32), the Vita-Kombi 1 (£49), the Vita-A-Kombi 3 Spot Zapper (£21), and the Oxygen Face Cream (£35)'. In a conversation with Style.com, Cichocki also confirmed that the company is 'in talks with Clarence House about doing the beauty for the bridal party'. They provided a similar service for guests at the 2002 wedding reception of fashion designer Stella McCartney, when the company's 'aestheticians' (known as beauticians to Brits) were employed to pamper guests.

When Komy met Kate

Though much of the attention focused on her hair, it's worth reiterating that on the day her engagement was announced, and in the subsequent official photos taken by legendary fashion photographer Mario Testino, Kate Middleton looked beautiful. Her make-up was understated and sophisticated, with no particular feature being emphasised, which accentuated her suitably ladylike image. Commentators soon began speculating about who exactly had achieved such results, only to be surprised when it was confirmed that the future Queen of England did her own make-up, and did it well. But how did that come to be? Photos of Kate as a teenager show a sporty-looking girl, with little interest in make-up. At St Andrews, where she was christened 'the prettiest girl on campus', she was able to rely on her natural beauty.

It was only after graduating and moving into London's increased media glare that she sought the help of a professional make-up artist, Komal 'Komy' Singh, to help her create a more groomed image. Though not famous, Singh is well-known in fashion circles, having worked on photo shoots for magazines such as *Vogue* and *W*.

Many young women thrust into the spotlight would have considered hiring someone to help them in this way, but it is telling that Kate did not want Komy to be her full-time make-up artist. Instead, demonstrating a practical streak that could have come straight from Princess Anne, but is undoubtedly the result of having self-made parents, Kate hired Komy to give her make-up lessons.

Karen Clarkson and Rebecca English, The Daily Mail

By learning which products suit her, and how to apply them, Kate has managed to ensure that there has never been a truly awful 'Kate Without Make-Up' photo splashed across the tabloids. The fact that she reportedly spends twenty minutes re-doing her make-up before leaving nightclubs has no doubt helped her avoid such a scenario.

In November 2010 Buckingham Palace confirmed that the new Princess-in-waiting had yet to appoint a full-time make-up artist, as she's expected to when – after her wedding – she begins attending public events as part of her royal duties. Komy Singh, one suspects, is keeping her fingers crossed.

Official Engagement Portraits

Kate's effortlessly natural look in Testino's engagement portraits shows how well she has taken on board Komy's training. Though Kate's look is founded on her natural beauty, it is one that – like her hairstyle – will have taken time and effort.

Although she is more made up than usual in the engagement shots, Kate has not drastically changed her look. She will have started her day as usual by cleansing, toning and moisturising with her favourite Karin Herzog products. Next she has clearly applied a primer – a luminising product that goes under foundation – which gives her skin its glowy, fresh look. After this she has applied foundation in a colour that exactly matches her skin tone. Knowing that she is about to face a camera, she will have applied foundation all over; normally, she would just apply it to some areas in order to even out her skin tone. She has probably also employed a little concealer to cover up any blemishes so that her look is truly flawless. To this base Kate adds bronzer, which she has swept along the length of her cheekbone using a wide brush, before applying a spot of blusher onto the apple of her cheeks. Kate keeps her eye make-up simple, using a dark grey eyeliner to circle her entire eye and a touch of French Grey eyeshadow. After this she has probably applied a little under-eye concealer, lighter than the one used on her skin, and framed her eyes with a coat of mascara. She finishes off her look with a nude lipstick.

Get the Look: Natural Make-up

The key words to keep in mind are: understated, unembarrassing and classic. So, whenever you think about applying a little bit more mascara, lip gloss or rouge, think again.

You will need:

Really good hair
As discussed, thick, glossy bounciness such as Kate has is hard to recreate at home, but a deep-conditioning treatment, volumising shampoo and conditioner, root-lift spray, hairdryer, rollers, bristle brush, and lots of patience and practice will help.

Radiant skin
Admittedly, a significant part of Kate's healthy glow comes from the sheer joy of knowing that her patience has indeed been a virtue and she's finally being rewarded with marriage to the love of her life, who also happens to be the future King of England. That said, you can encourage such enviable radiance either by using Karin Herzog's pricey, oxygen-infused products or a lower-priced radiance-boosting moisturiser.

Really good make-up
While there's been no word on what make-up brands Kate actually favours, radiance-enhancing foundation and primers never do a girl-about-town any harm. Nor does blusher, bronzer, highlighter, blemish concealer, under-eye concealer (yes, they're different), blotting powder or a sister who's quick to point out any visible flaws that may have emerged so you can cover them up quickly.

A nude lip
If it's a very special occasion – such as an official engagement photograph – you may even supplement your natural loveliness with a lipstick, which should also be in a nude shade from a respectable brand. No red, however.

Or even a wee bit of lip gloss
But never too much and only in very, very natural tones.

Lessons from a professional make-up artist
Don't worry if you can't afford an internationally renowned one. Many make-up companies give free lessons at their counters.

Fake tan
Kate and her sister Pippa are both devotees of St Tropez sunless tanning treatments, which they top up when holidaying with friends in Kenya and Mustique.

A manicure
According to reports, Kate regularly spends £55 on manicures at Richard Ward's Metrospa, favouring nude shades such as pale pink. A word to the wise: these should *never*, *ever* be French-tipped.

Whether she's attending Nelson Mandela's 90th Birthday concert in Hyde Park, or announcing her engagement to the world, Kate's hair and make-up is always elegant, understated and classic-looking.

> ❝ I call this stealth make-up. It ensures you look fabulous but not too made up. Kate has already mastered this natural make-up look. ❞
>
> *Jemma Kidd*

Pretty hands

Now she's finally got the ring, Kate will want to keep her hands in good condition, all the better to show it off. Julie Cichocki from Karin Herzog recommends that Kate use 'our moisturising Hand & Nail Cream (£36)', because 'beautiful, white clean nails are every bit as important as youthful-looking skin'.

Partially tamed brows

A key to getting the natural look (which, in case you hadn't already guessed, takes hours and more products than many women will own in their lifetime), is really good eyebrows. You'll notice that Kate's aren't over-plucked, particularly on top, creating a just-rolled-out-of-bed beauty which may well be down to professional advice.

Smoky but understated eye make-up

Grey eyeliner gives a softer, less dramatic look than black. Eyeliner should only be applied all around the eye on very special occasions. It is acceptable to use black mascara at all times, as long as you remember that you are soon to be royalty, and should thus refrain from over-exaggerating your lashes: *one coat is enough.*

Get the Exercise and Diet Regime

Even before she proved herself to be fit for a future king, Kate Middleton was sporty. At school she excelled at athletics, holding records for both high jump and long jump, and was also a star of the netball and hockey teams. After she left school, Kate added even more sporting activities to her schedule, becoming a keen rower and gym regular. When she split up with William for a brief time in 2007 she threw herself into rowing, joining the Sisterhood, an all-women's team who practiced in a traditional Chinese dragon boat on the River Thames. Kate was set to join the team when they became the first female crew to cross the English Channel – and were it not for paparazzi intrusion, she would surely have done so.

According to a 2008 report in *The Daily Mail*, Kate's devotion to staying fit is such that she asked Prince William to build a gym for her in Clarence House. 'She works out for at least an hour a day and loves to stay slim and toned,' a source claimed. In the run-up to her wedding, Kate has apparently been feeling pressure to work out even more, to make sure she looks her absolute best on the big day. In November 2010, *Radar Online* reported that '[the] 5'10" beauty has upped her daily hour-long gym workouts, which include cycling, jogging and light weights to ensure she keeps her 120lb body in shape.'

How Kate Keeps Fit

School netball and rounders teams
Kate played a lot of sport from a young age, which will have strengthened her muscles, giving her the perfect platform to stay fit later in life. Games like netball and hockey provide a good all-over body workout as players are constantly required to switch pace from a walk to a jog to a sprint, while shooting and passing strengthens arm and side muscles. These games will also have taught a young Kate how to be a team player – exactly the kind of quality the country needs from its future Queen.

Cycling in London
Kate enjoys exercise so much that she includes it in her daily routine whenever she can. Before the press attention became too much this included cycling through London during summertime. As well as improving her strength, stamina and cardiovascular fitness, by choosing two wheels over four, Kate was also doing her bit for the environment.

Rowing with the Sisterhood
Although her short split from William was a dark time in Kate's personal life, she never let it get in the way of her athleticism, joining the Sisterhood for early morning training sessions on the River Thames. Rowing is predominantly an aerobic sport, making it a fantastic way to burn fat, and it has certainly helped Kate maintain her incredible figure. Although you are unlikely to spot her on the river these days, Kate has a rowing machine in her house and spends at least half an hour a day on it. Crucially, even for an early morning on the Thames, Kate never abandons her grooming regime.

An enthusiastic cyclist and rower, Kate's enviably trim figure is a direct result of her active and health-conscious lifestyle.

Skiing

The first hint that the young couple were getting serious came in 2004, when Kate joined William and his family on their annual ski trip to Klosters. Kate was already an avid skier and this was to be the first of several excursions to the exclusive Swiss resort. Unlike most of us, who return from our holidays a few pounds heavier, Kate will have come away from her trips to Klosters even trimmer than when she arrived. A day's skiing will easily burn off any little indulgences (you can burn up to 3,000 calories in six hours) and it also exercises all of your major muscle groups.

Shooting

Like her future in-laws, Kate is keen on traditional country sports. Although less exuberant than her other sporting activities, a day spent walking in the fresh air will certainly help with her overall fitness. Even on a shoot, she keeps it stylish.

Going to the gym

In the past, Kate has used the Clarence House gym to do her hour-a-day workout in total privacy. However, Kate is said to have stepped up her regime since the announcement of her engagement and has recently joined the exclusive Harbour Club. A favourite haunt of Princess Diana's, the club is close to Kate's Chelsea pad and offers a state-of-the-art gym and daily classes, including yoga, tai chi and kickboxing. The club also provides individually tailored programmes to help brides-to-be get in shape for their big day, and Kate may well take advantage of this service. If the stress of planning a wedding gets too much, she can always relax in the club spa.

Kate's Diet

As she's slimmed down over the past few years, Kate's diet has come under increasing scrutiny, with concerns that, like Princess Diana before her, she may have succumbed to an eating disorder. Her mother Carole has spoken publicly about following the Dukan Diet which, in short, promotes eating a lot of protein and very few complex carbohydrates in order to lose weight, prompting speculation that Kate too may be munching her way through vast amounts of prawns, cottage cheese and sausages in order to stay trim. In fact, Kate's energetic lifestyle means that she burns enough calories not to have to rely upon faddy diets. Friends of the Princess-in-waiting confirm that she eats three healthy meals a day and is careful to make sure that the balance of carbohydrates, protein and fibre in each is correct.

Breakfast is often porridge, muesli or wholegrain brown toast with tea.
Lunch is lean meat or fish served with a salad or vegetables.
Dinner, shared with William, is usually a similarly healthy choice like chicken or salmon with plenty of vegetables. Kate often steams her food – this healthy method of cooking maintains flavour and preserves nutrients without adding fat. Of course, every now and then she treats herself; she has been seen popping pizza into her supermarket basket and sometimes cooks less-than-healthy British classics like William's favourite, shepherd's pie.
Snacks are not a big part of Kate's diet. She usually chooses fruit, nuts, yoghurt and the odd bit of dark chocolate if she needs anything else to get her through the day.
Drinks are also few and far between. Although she was fond of cocktails in her clubbing days, friends say she now gets through nights out on a single glass of wine – a healthy habit that's bound to keep her calorie intake low.

Kate joins the royal ski party on the slopes at Klosters, Switzerland, in March 2005.

Kate: Sloane on the Slopes

❝ Sweet, sensible and stylish, this girl won't be caught
without her hot pink Bollé goggles in a blizzard. ❞

Ticky Hedley-Dent, The Daily Mail

Amongst her other sporting accomplishments, Kate shows considerable skill on the slopes. Like every other Sloane-friendly sport, skiing comes with a certain sense of style.

How to achieve Kate's skiing style

Separates

All-in-ones were the height of slope style in the eighties but it's safe to say this is no longer the case. Kate is usually kitted out in good quality, well-matched separates in classic colours like red and black. In recent years she has ditched her somewhat utilitarian red Schoffel ski-jacket for a fitted white one with detachable faux-fur collar from luxury British skiwear brand E+O. When the weather's warmer your jacket can be replaced with a padded gilet.

Eye-wear

If the weather's good, your usual Chanel sunglasses will do the trick – but wearing them in the snow is something of a safety hazard. When the weather turns on you, bring out your Bollé goggles – in a coordinating colour – and regain your sight without losing your style.

Hats and hair

Kate often wears her hair loose for skiing, letting it flow out behind her as she shoots down the slopes. Although the weather sometimes forces even Kate Middleton to don a sensible bobble hat, crucially we have yet to see her with hat hair.

Après-ski

Kate opts for chunkier knitwear than she would normally wear. She will usually wear a thick wool jumper, layered under a fleece or gilet with jeans or ski joggers tucked into sheepskin or faux-fur lined boots.

❝ They have interests in common: They can go skiing together,
play together, not just do his stuff and her stuff but our stuff. ❞

Lissa Coffey, relationship expert and author.

Kate retains her elegant but practical style on the slopes of Klosters, Switzerland, while holidaying with the royal family in 2005 (top left and right). The royal couple share a tender moment in the snow during a holiday in Zermatt, Switzerland, March 2007 (bottom left) and (right) Kate and Prince William ride a drag lift up the mountainside of Klosters in March 2008 .

Kate: Party at the Polo

❛This year, when Kate came to the match, I caught them standing with their friends and they looked so relaxed and friendly. I said to my son that I hope they get married soon because I could see they are made for each other. ❜

Saroj Chakravarty, a friend of HRH Prince Charles who organises annual polo matches with the royal family.

To look good at Polo matches is to strike a careful balance between smart and casual. The look hinges on looking both well put together and groomed but also like you haven't tried very hard at all. As such, it's not too far away from Kate's everyday look.

Floaty summer dresses

Kate's favourite floaty summer dresses are perfect for the smart-casual polo look. Be careful not to wear too short a skirt – your day will probably involve sitting on the grass.

Dark jeans

Jeans are permissible but they should be skinny and in a smart shade such as navy. Wear with blouses; not t-shirts.

A touch of leather

Leather is perfect for cooler days at the polo; it adds a touch of style to your outfit – it's also warm and waterproof. On various occasions Kate has been spotted in a black leather jacket and also – on chilly days – in a brown suede gilet with matching gloves and boots.

(Polo) Ralph Lauren

It's in the name. Ralph Lauren's cable knit jumpers are perfect smart-casual polo wear.

Sensible shoes

Fashionistas beware: the polo is not the time to break out your favourite pair of Manolos as they'll only sink into the grass. Wear flat shoes or a pair of wedges so you can participate in the tradition of 'stomping the divots', as shown in the film *Pretty Woman*. Women who attend polo matches help replace the divots (mounds of grass that the horses have kicked away from the soil during the match) by stomping them back into place.

Left and opposite: When attending polo matches over the years, Kate has always struck the perfect balance between smart and casual.

Chapter 6

A Right Royal Engagement

'I really didn't expect it at all. It was a **total shock** when it came, and I was very excited.'

Kate Middleton, 16 November 2010

On the day her engagement was announced, Kate Middleton looked radiant. Pictures of the Princess-in-waiting and her husband-to-be looking ecstatically happy and very much in love were published around the world on the day their betrothal was publicly confirmed. Apart from her appearance on her wedding day, Kate's engagement look may well be the most important of her life.

The Ring

'It's a family ring. It's my mother's engagement ring. I thought it would be quite nice because obviously she's not going to be around to share in the excitement of it all – this is my way of keeping her close to it all. '

Prince William, 16 November 2010

Never has the legacy of Princess Diana and her doomed marriage to Prince Charles seemed to sit more heavily on Kate Middleton's shoulders than when she began wearing the late Princess of Wales's engagement ring. Naysayers pointed to the old wives' tale that jewellery collects the luck of its previous owners and that – in terms of the fairytale gone wrong – no one had it worse than Diana, whose early marriage led to battles with eating disorders and depression before her divorce and untimely death. Why, they wondered, would William cast that shadow over his own marriage and bride-to-be?

In simple terms the answer seems to be that Prince William is not superstitious, and he is sentimental enough to want to include his late mother in his wedding celebrations. Her engagement ring seems the most obvious symbol of not only how much he loves his future wife, but also how much he misses his mother, and how he, like Diana, believes in the fairytale.

The royal engagement ring is made up of a dazzling eighteen-carat oval sapphire that is surrounded by a series of smaller diamonds. Though it is now considered an heirloom, the ring was unusual when given to Princess Diana as, rather than being specially commissioned, it was bought from a jeweller, meaning that anyone who could afford the £28,000 price tag could also buy one.

Prince Charles and Princess Diana's fairytale beginning.

Famously, Princess Diana wore this ring, the symbol of the fairytale romance she never stopped believing in, until her death in 1997.

❜Diana chose her [engagement ring] two days before the official announcement when a tray of twelve was sent by Garrard to Windsor Castle where, after dinner, she, Charles and the Queen all gathered to make the choice. The ring cost £28,000 [£250,000 in today's money] and the Queen paid for it.❜

Hello! *magazine*

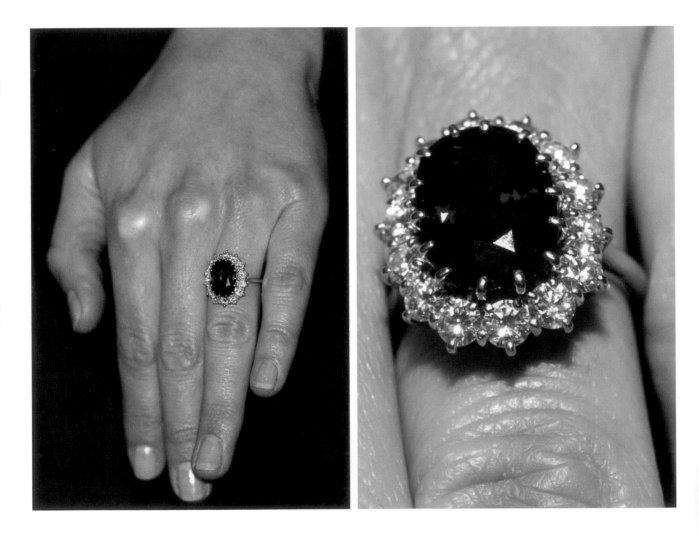

Previously worn by Princess Diana, Kate's dazzling engagement ring features an eighteen-carat oval sapphire surrounded by a series of smaller diamonds.

The Dress

When Kate and William publicly announced their engagement, Kate wore what quickly became referred to as 'that dress', an honour that is rarely conferred upon dresses in this paparazzi-dominated era of here-today, gone-tomorrow fashion. The appropriately named 'Sapphire' dress by Issa, one of Kate's favourite labels, was bought off the peg at Fenwick's Bond Street store for the sum of £385, and perfectly matched the sapphire in her engagement ring. While some members of the fashion press sneered over this 'matchy-matchyness' (a style no-no, according to Anna Wintour, the legendary editor of American *Vogue*), the public disagreed, deeming it a style triumph from a young woman preparing for a lifetime in the public eye. Harvey Nichols sold out of the silk and jersey gathered-front dress within twenty-four hours, and high-street tributes from shops such as Coast, Lipsy, Tesco and Peacock's were soon gone too. The dress was also a sell-out in the US – even *Saturday Night Live* couldn't get hold of one for their royal engagement sketch, in which Anne Hathaway played Miss Middleton. A replica of the dress had to be made by the show's wardrobe department.

> ‘Given her fabulous figure, it can't be hard to find something that she'd look good in. But, while it looks figure-hugging, the sapphire blue, silk jersey dress would suit most women.’
>
> The Daily Mail, *25 November 2010*

American fashion designer Michael Kors, who is known for his classic and elegant designs, may have summed up the public's feelings towards the Princess-in-waiting when he told Vogue.com that, 'When Barack Obama first became well known and everyone started looking at Mrs Obama I thought to myself, "This is a very different, modern-looking couple." When I look at Kate I see a changing of the guard in what is considered elegant. She likes to look easy but chic. I would liken her to Obama and Carla Bruni in that way. All these women are in situations where they [are] shaking off the formal suits of their predecessors.'

Another political wife who springs to mind when one considers Kate's personal style is Jacqueline Kennedy Onassis, whose timelessly elegant style, which never succumbed to faddish trends, remains remarkable even today, putting Kate in well-dressed company.

Issa: Kate's Favourite Label

' It was a total surprise when she wore it. We were in the office when I got an email saying, "She's wearing Issa." And then it went insane. The phones went crazy, every TV station in the world wanted to interview me. In the shops, people went mad and it wasn't just that dress that sold out, but Issa in general. All over the world. In Japan, they went crazy; in Brazil, they went crazy; in America, they went crazy; everywhere. For my business it has been the Midas touch. '

Daniella Issa Helayel

Daniella Issa Helayel, a Brazilian-born designer who's now based in London, founded Kate's favourite fashion label Issa in 2001, when she couldn't find a dress that could take her from work to the beach to a party. Described by Jess Cartner-Morley, fashion editor of *The Guardian*, as being 'known for flattering, don't-frighten-the-horses frocks: one part international chic in the style of Diane Von Furstenberg's wrap dresses, one part Fulham yummy mummy', the label's fashion shows are often attended by Kate's sister Pippa, while Princesses Eugenie and Beatricehave also been known to put in catwalk-side appearances.

Left: This gorgeous sapphire dress by Issa became a must-have item for women around the world when Kate was photographed wearing it at the official engagement announcement on 16 November 2010. Right: Leaving her Chelsea home for work in August 2007. Centre: Kate attends the 2007 Concert for Diana in a 'white-hot' Issa trench coat and black knee-high boots. Far right: Kate steps out in a stunning black Issa number during her brief separation from William, June 2007.

The Engagement Portraits

❛ For much of their eight-year courtship they abided by a pact not to touch in public, conscious that their every move was subject to scrutiny and speculation. Now, nearly a month after Prince William and Kate announced their engagement, we see them for the first time just as they wish to be seen: a young couple bursting with happiness and love; intimate and at ease and unlike any royal couple before. **❜**

The Daily Mail

Kate and William's engagement portraits were published on 13 December 2010. Unusually, the royal couple had commissioned two, both of which were taken by Mario Testino, who had been Princess Diana's favourite photographer. Though the press sniped because Testino had indulged in his customary airbrushing of the photographs, no one could deny that the couple they showed seemed to be very much in love.

The first featured the young couple from head to waist, smiling at the camera. William had his arms wrapped around Kate, whose left hand rested just so on her husband-to-be's arm, showing off her beautiful engagement ring.

One of the most relaxed engagement photos ever published by the royal family showed the couple looking gorgeous in creamy tones, with Kate having raided her wardrobe for a Whistles silk blouse that cost £95 in the company's Autumn/Winter 2008 collection. In response to Kate wearing the blouse, Jane Shepherdson, CEO of Whistles, decided to re-issue it, saying, 'We are delighted that Catherine has chosen to wear Whistles in her engagement photographs. Due to a surge of customer interest we will be re-releasing the "Kate" blouse as a limited edition in early 2011.'

The second, more formal, portrait was taken in the Council Chamber of St James's Palace. The couple are standing close together. William has a hand resting on Kate's waist, with Kate's left hand lightly touching it, again to show off her engagement ring. In this picture, Kate is wearing a dress that came from her own wardrobe and was, like her blouse, purchased from an upper-end high-street

One of fashion photographer Mario Testino's official engagement portraits of the royal couple.

shop – this time Reiss. David Reiss, the founder and managing director of the chain, was thrilled that Kate chose a Reiss dress for the photograph, saying, 'Kate has been a customer of Reiss for some time now and we are absolutely delighted that she chose to wear one of our dresses for such a wonderful occasion.' He confirmed that a similar version of Kate's white 'Nannette' dress, which cost £159, would be sold in Reiss stores at the end of January 2011. The earrings Kate wore in both pictures were white topaz 'Hope' droplets by Links of London, which cost £275. It was confirmed that, as on the day her engagement was announced, the Princess-in-waiting had done her own make-up for both portraits, though Testino made sure his own make-up artist was on hand, just in case they were needed.

Mario Testino

Born in Lima, Peru, Mario Testino is an internationally famous fashion photographer who has worked for magazines such as *Vogue*, *Vanity Fair* and *V*. He is well-known for his celebrity portraits, having photographed subjects such as Madonna, Julia Roberts, Margaret Thatcher and, most famously, the *Vanity Fair* portraits of Princess Diana at Kensington Palace in 1997. The Princess of Wales said that Testino's photographs of her were the most beautiful she had ever felt. 'She said to me at the time [that] her children had said to her it was the most "her" they had seen,' the photographer later revealed, perhaps explaining how he has retained such a close bond with the family, having produced birthday portraits of both William and Harry (for their twenty-first and twentieth birthdays, respectively).

❛ I have photographed Prince William several times officially, but never Catherine Middleton. I already felt confident that she would be an easy sitter, as she has natural grace, a very open personality, and a beautiful face and posture. I had noticed how beautiful she usually looks in the press and how stylish she is, with a preference for simpler clothes that show off her great figure, and it was a real treat to photograph her. ❜

Mario Testino

William and Kate support the English team in London during the RBS Six Nations Championship match between England and Italy, 10 February 2007.

Chapter 7

A Dress to Impress

'The first thing her designer must remember is that though they are creating something that will be seen by millions, there is only one person who needs to be happy with it: Kate.'

Elizabeth Emanuel, designer of Princess Diana's iconic wedding gown

The Dress

*❜ Well, I'm here in Chelsea, I design for that set . . . hopefully people
think it's me because they think I design beautiful things
[but] we haven't been asked to do anything. ❜*

Phillipa Lepley

A new title will be bestowed upon Kate the moment she marries. But for many
people the true confirmation of her status will come when they see her in
her wedding dress. On 20 December 2010 *The Huffington Post* reported that the
dressmaking process had begun in Buckingham Palace under maximum security;
they could not confirm which designer had been chosen, hinting only that they
were British and not yet well known.

Speaking to *The Telegraph* in November 2010, Elizabeth Emanuel, who came to
prominence when she and her ex-husband David made Princess Diana's wedding
dress, explained, 'The most important thing [the designer] will have to worry about
is security, because secrecy is the really big issue. We had to have a huge safe hauled
in through the windows of our studio and the dress was locked away every night.
We had two security guards twenty-four hours a day and only one person, apart
from David and myself, ever worked on the dress.'

By keeping the dress inside the palace walls, it has been kept under the ultimate
form of lock and key, preserving both Kate and her designer's privacy, and offering
them greater security, as even the most desperate paparazzi photographers are
highly unlikely to try and break into the palace for a snap of the unfinished dress,
however valuable such an image might be.

Immediately after the royal engagement was announced, speculation over who
would make Kate's dress began, with commentators such as celebrity stylist Kate
Halfpenny opining that, 'Her dress will be the polar opposite to Diana's. It will be
simple, elegant and effortless. It will let her shine rather than swamp her.'

Although it would be highly unusual for a British princess to choose a foreign
designer, that didn't stop everyone from celebrity-favourite Vera Wang to Chanel's
German-born couturier Karl Lagerfeld, revered French fashion designer Christian

Prince William's parents Charles and Diana on their wedding day, 29 July 1981.

Vera Wang   Karl Lagerfeld   Badgley Mischka

Christian Lacroix

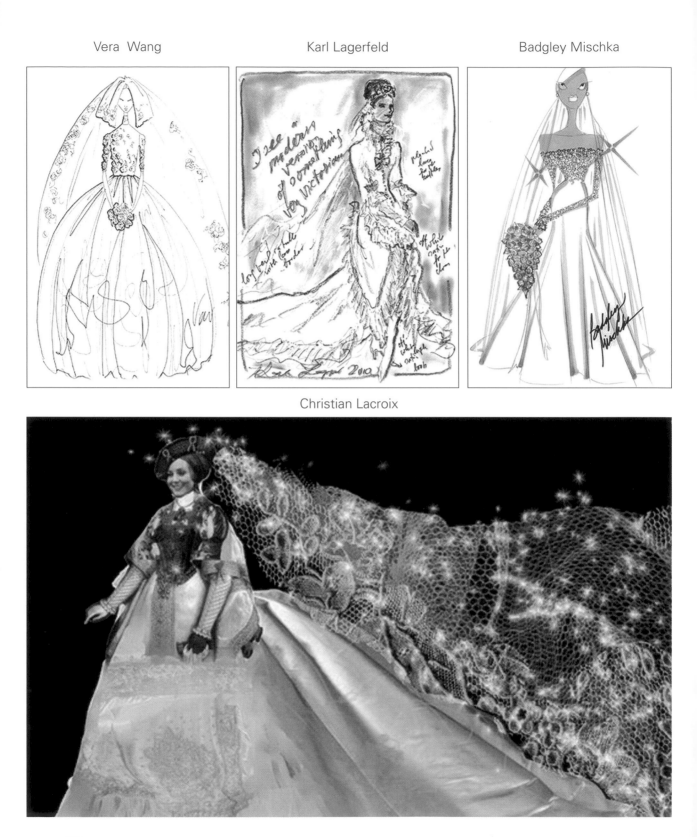

Lacroix and American fashion duo Badgley Mischka from submitting designs. Wang made the future Queen look like a beautiful doll, while Lagerfeld's playful design included a gown 'open in the front' to be worn with high boots, and Lacroix played on the royal theme by incorporating an Elizabethan-style bodice.

Badgley Mischka's proposal, however, took the cake: they suggested Kate wear an open-shouldered fish-tail gown encrusted with jewels from neckline to waist. There were no words.

The Contenders

Bruce Oldfield

A favourite designer and good friend of Princess Diana, bookies actually closed betting on who would design Kate's dress because Oldfield proved such a popular choice. Oldfield himself 'simply couldn't comment' but he did disclose that he would be designing dresses for 'a huge amount' of guests.

❛ She also has such a gorgeous figure that she would look stunning in anything. I would play to all of these points and design a simple silhouette with sufficient detailing to give it a sense of occasion but not so much as to drown her slight frame . . . Her dress might be traditional and elegant, possibly even demure, but I'm sure she would want a modern twist; a nod to fashion. ❜

Bruce Oldfield

Phillipa Lepley

The original bookies' favourite, Lepley has a reputation for understated elegance, which should suit Kate perfectly. The Chelsea-based designer is favoured by well-to-do London brides and has dressed a number of William and Kate's friends.

Issa

The designer of Kate's engagement dress refuses to be drawn, saying only: 'I don't talk about wedding dresses! I've no idea what she will choose. It will be a surprise for all of us [but Kate] knows what suits her. She has effortless glamour and she works that very well. And I think she's absolutely right to keep it a secret – it's cool.'

Left: Women's Wear Daily *asked designers to imagine Kate's wedding dress.*

'She does wear very slinky things. She could go quite traditional, but I think she will show off her body; everything she's worn so far points to that. She's a lucky girl; she has the most amazing hair and figure and smile, so I'm sure she will get it right.'

Phillipa Lepley

Libélula

One of Kate's favourite labels (stocked in King's Road boutique, Austique) is Libélula. Designed by Sophie Cranston, who has worked for Temperley and McQueen, the little-known newcomers are set to start producing bespoke wedding dresses in 2011. Could Kate be their first customer?

Sassi Holford

The self-taught dressmaker designed Autumn Kelly's dress for her wedding to the Queen's eldest grandson in May 2008. Sophistication and modesty are her hallmarks.

Amanda Wakeley

Another close friend and favourite of the Princess of Wales, Wakeley was awarded an OBE for her services to fashion in 2010.

Alice Temperley

Boho designer Temperley is a favourite of the international fashion crowd, and Kate has sported Temperley's dresses and clutch bags on numerous occasions. However, Alice confirmed: 'We're definitely not doing it. We know she shops in our discount store at Bicester, so I tried to send a message to her through a friend with my number, but I don't know if it even got to her.'

Julien MacDonald

When interviewed the Welsh wonder, who specialises in making luxuriously spangly dresses, said, 'Kate's dress would have to befit her beauty and classic taste, the place where the ceremony would take place as well as the worldwide audience. I see her in a beautiful, intricately ornate yet simple and romantic dress in a shade of white. I would love to design it.'

Wearing this black and cream Alice Temperley dress with an embellished neckline and black jacket, Kate was a guest of honour at the Teenage Cancer Trust Christmas Spectacular on 18 December 2010 – her and William's first public appearance together following the announcement of their engagement.

meetings in unusual locations, decoy dresses and midnight fittings. When designing Diana's dress, Elizabeth and David Emanuel would refer to Diana by the name 'Debra' in the studio. In 1981 the paparazzi were more gentlemanly than now, but the young designers were still followed everywhere in cabs.

Like Diana, Kate is every designer's dream. Unlike Diana, who was 19 at the time she got engaged, Kate's more fashion-savvy. Quietly, slowly, she's also been having a sleekover for months: getting dresses made for social occasions in order to avoid turning up in the same dress as anyone else, often by her favourite designer Daniella Helayel of Issa. She already has all the makings of a future fashion icon too – the £385 Issa London dress Kate wore to the engagement press

conference promptly sold out at Harvey Nichols in just 24 hours.

Kate's developed a style that is essentially 'playing it safe'. Her hemline is never too short; her neckline is never too low. Diana, however, made mistakes: even with her wedding dress, which was crumpled and, scandalously, bared her shoulders – considered 'inappropriate' in the hallowed surrounds of St Paul's.

Stewart Parvin, dressmaker by appointment to the Queen and top of Debret's recommendations list, says protocol must be observed. 'Most brides want to be strapless: but this is not an option for a royal bride. It is not about being sexy – it's about being sophisticated and regal. I would suggest a long train, a hint of cleavage, but nothing more.' Royal dress-iquotte also dictates the designer must be British. The Emanuels sourced ▶

THE FASHION SHORTLIST

We asked these top British designers to illustrate their fantasy royal wedding dress

PREEN

SASSI HOLFORD

GRAEME BLACK

Kate dashiel after 2011

ROKSANDA ILINCIC

JULIEN MACDONALD

KATE'S CROWNING GLORY

KATE MIDDLETON doesn't have family tiaras – we're assuming the 'Princess Sequin Tiara Crown' sold on her family's Party Pieces website for £3.99 doesn't count! So she will have to be lent one – this will be her 'something borrowed' (the 'something blue' is that sapphire engagement ring!). Our etiquette expert, royal-appointed fashion designer Stewart Parvin, tells us that Kate will 'immediately inherit a tiara at the moment she marries' and not a moment before – both the Duchess of York and Countess of Wessex arrived wearing flowers in their hair, but reappeared wearing tiaras after the signing of the register. So which of the royal family's extensive collection of priceless tiaras will Kate wear? Here are the contenders.

by Garrard's in 1914 for Queen Mary.

GRAND DUCHESS 'GIRLS OF GREAT BRITAIN AND IRELAND' TIARA
This tiara was created as a wedding gift for Princess May of Teck (later known as Queen Mary).

QUEEN ALEXANDRA'S KOKOSHNIK TIARA
Queen Alexandra, the wife of King Edward VII, commissioned Garrard's to create this tiara in the style of a Russian peasant's headdress. It is composed of 61 platinum bars and 488 diamonds. It is frequently worn by the Queen.

THE KING GEORGE VI TIARA
Worn by Princess Elizabeth and Princess Anne on their wedding days.

THE SPENCER TIARA (FAMILY HEIRLOOM ABOVE)
Princess Diana borrowed this to wear on her wedding day.

THE CAMBRIDGE LOVER'S KNOT TIARA (OPTION)
Frequently worn by Diana. The tiara was given to her by the Queen. It was created

23

Here Comes the GOWN

THE WAIT FOR THEIR ENGAGEMENT IS OVER, BUT THE WORLD IS ANTICIPATING... THE DRESS OF THE CENTURY. WHAT WILL **KATE** WEAR TO WED **PRINCE WILLIAM**?

The moment **Prince William** and **Kate Middleton** announced their engagement, the question was What will the princess bride wear? Now they've set a date (April 29) and a venue (Westminster Abbey), so Kate is ready to select a designer and begin the elaborate process of creating her gown. Of course, it's more than a wedding dress; it will be a symbol of her transformation from commoner Kate to Princess Catherine, and will define her public image.

"This dress has to be perfect," renowned British designer Bruce Oldfield tells OK! "A hand-crafted piece of couture, using only the best materials; nothing about the fit or finish can be left to chance. It will be a part of history!"

In fact, an estimated billion-plus people around the world are expected to watch the televised affair.

WHO'S THE LUCKY DESIGNER?
Kate will keep her dress secret until the wedding, but her choice of designer is expected to be announced soon. British designers Phillipa Lepley and Oldfield (a Diana favorite) are said to top the list, but Daniella Issa Helayel, who created Kate's blue engagement dress, is also a contender. The sentimental choice is

Elizabeth Emanuel, who, with her ex-husband, David, designed Princess Diana's wedding gown.

KATE CALLS THE SHOTS
Despite the importance of this dress, the queen won't have the final say: "Kate decides — with help from her mother," a royal insider tells OK! In fact Kate's father might be the one who pays for the gown, estimated to cost up to $250,000.

Still, Kate will be advised by Palace aides on protocol: Bare shoulders and anything too slinky are a no-no at sacred Westminster Abbey.

Kate and the aides are meeting with dressmakers. The chosen one will work with a small, trusted staff and take security measures such as private garbage collection (to keep the curious from finding fabric scraps) and guards to protect their studio, explains Camilla Tominey, royal editor of British newspaper the *Sunday Express*, and OK!'s royal expert in London. After all, the Palace can't afford mishaps when it comes to the gown of the century.

"It's going to be a challenge," says designer Elizabeth, "It's a royal occasion, a historical moment. It's got to be something that really reflects that."

Kate and William plan to invite 100 randomly selected members of the public to the wedding.

'If I was entrusted with [designing Kate's dress], it would be a huge privilege'

—Elizabeth Emanuel, who designed Princess Diana's royal wedding dress in 1981

THE BACK

Elizabeth Emanuel

DESIGNER ELIZABETH EMANUEL GIVES OK! THIS EXCLUSIVE SKETCH OF KATE'S DREAM DRESS
"Kate has developed her own sense of style. She very much knows what suits her," says Elizabeth Emanuel. "I would imagine she would go for something quite simple. I'm pretty certain [it's] not going to look like Diana's dress.

"The most important thing is to do an absolutely amazing dress for the bride," Elizabeth explains. "The bride is the most important part of this at the end of the day. And... billions of people [are] watching, as well."

OK! WWW.OKMAGAZINE.COM

Valentino   Ben De Lisi

Jenny Packham

The award-winning designer is a favourite of brides-to-be up and down the country, specialising in elegant designs, often with a vintage twist.

Stewart Parvin

Designer by appointment to the Queen, Parvin understands that, 'Most brides want [their dress] to be strapless; but this is not an option for a royal bride. It is not about being sexy, it's about being sophisticated and regal. I would suggest a long train, a hint of cleavage, but nothing more.'

Vivienne Westwood

The Grand Dame of British Fashion makes ready use of royal and monarchical imagery in her collections but is perhaps too radical a choice for Kate.

A number of publications including Grazia *(opposite above),* OK! *(opposite below),* Women's Wear Daily *(above left) and* Hello! *(above right) asked designers to sketch their ideal wedding dress for Kate.*

Chapter 8

On Her Wedding Day

❛ So Cinderella married the Prince, and in time they came to be King and Queen, and lived happily ever after. ❜

Cinderella

It's pleasing to paint Kate Middleton as a real-life equivalent to Cinderella, a fairytale beauty who rose from commoner to princess. But it's hard to imagine that during her stolidly middle-class childhood, Kate or her parents ever really thought that she would end up marrying a prince, with all the pomp and splendour that accompanies such a match. On her wedding day, Kate will show the world that she is ready to become a member of the royal family. Her sense of style will be emphasised by her wedding dress. She has apparently encouraged Prince William to marry her wearing his RAF regimental uniform that she has described as 'so sexy', proving that not even a Princess-in-waiting can resist a man in uniform.

In 2010, the average British wedding cost £25,000. Kate Middleton's parents are expected to contribute £100,000 towards their eldest daughter's 2011 nuptials, most of which has apparently been allotted to covering the price of her wedding dress. The day's overall cost is estimated at five million pounds, something the British government are hoping will be more than covered by the tourism it generates, not that they're too worried – even in times of recession, the government has contingency plans in place to cover the expenditure necessary for a large and internationally important event such as this. In addition to the pressure to follow royal protocol, Kate is faced with massive media pressure. In November 2010, the press learned that she had increased her already stringent workout routine to ensure she'd be slim on her wedding day. She was both criticised and praised for this: she was labelled either a poor role model for succumbing to pressure to be thin, or a good role model for encouraging young women to exercise – proving that, whatever she does, she will never be able to please everyone. Debate about the bride on her wedding day will not be limited to who her dress is by. Her weight, hairstyle, make-up and choice of bridesmaids' dresses will all be placed under harsh scrutiny, and there's no escaping the fact that the happiest day of Kate's life will also be one of the most nerve-wracking.

> ‘All parties involved in the wedding, not least Prince William and Kate Middleton, want to ensure that a balance is struck between an enjoyable day and the current economic situation. ’
>
> *Jamie Lowther-Pinkerton, private secretary to Prince William, who has been in charge of wedding arrangements*

Kate once again makes a perfectly judged sartorial choice, pictured here with William after the Prince's graduation ceremony at RAF Cranwell on 11 April 2008.

Kate's Big Day in Four Easy Steps

Some Things Old

A silver sixpence

The last sixpence coins were minted in 1967, but for years before that, British brides customarily wore a sixpence coin in their shoe on their wedding day to bless their marriage with wealth and prosperity. Though we can assume that Kate and Wills will be able to live comfortably regardless, this is still a sweet tradition that Kate might want to embrace.

Her engagement ring

The sapphire heirloom ring, which belonged to Princess Diana, was made in 1981, thirty years before Kate and William's wedding.

Some Things New

Her wedding dress

The most anticipated dress of the year will be newly made to Kate's exact specifications. A fairytale princess could not ask for more.

Her wedding ring

Ever since the late Queen Mother married King George VI in 1923, royal wedding rings have been made of Welsh gold from the Clogau St David mine in Bontddu, North-West Wales. Princess Diana's was the last of the royal wedding rings to be made from the exact nugget of gold used for the Queen Mother's ring, of which only a sliver now remains. In 1981 the Royal British Legion presented the Queen with a thirty-six-gram nugget of twenty-one-carat gold to be used for future royal wedding rings, and it is expected that Kate and William's wedding bands will be made from this piece.

A tiara

A new tiara may be commissioned especially for Kate, as happened with Sarah Ferguson and Sophie Rhys-Jones. She will receive this the moment she marries, and like Sarah and Sophie is likely to leave the Abbey wearing it, after entering with flowers in her hair. Princess Diana too, was given a tiara on her wedding day; the Cambridge Lover's Knot was the Queen's wedding present to Diana.

If she's going fluid she will need lots of layers of fabric. You can't just do a little train, you need a big train. And obviously something very beautiful and spectacular. When you see those pictures of the red carpet outside, it's such a huge thing and she's going to be this little figure, so she needs to be pretty grand.

Phillipa Lepley

Some Things Borrowed

A tiara
If a tiara is not specially made for Kate, it's likely that she will be lent one by the royal family. It is even possible that the Spencer family will lend her the Spencer Tiara Diana wore when she entered St Paul's Cathedral on her wedding day.

Her mother's jewellery
Some brides have a piece of their mother's jewellery sewn into their dress for luck. This charming tradition may appeal to Kate, who is very close to her mother.

A veil
Rumour has it that Kate is considering wearing Princess Diana's cathedral-length veil when she walks up the aisle.

Some Things Blue

Her sapphire engagement ring
She may once again match it with the blue sapphire earrings she wore when her engagement was announced.

A blue ribbon
As with their mother's jewellery, many brides sew a blue ribbon into the inside of their dress for luck.

A garter
Not that the public will ever see it, but many a young bride has worn a garter with a blue ribbon attached on their wedding day.

Blue flowers
As blue is one of Kate's favourite colours, she may include these in her bouquet or wear them in her hair.

Princess Diana wearing the Spencer Tiara during a royal tour of Australia, April 1983.

Princess Brides

‘ Nevermind the vows . . . what did the bride wear? ’

Almost every fairytale ends with the image of a beautiful princess bride marrying her prince in order to live happily ever after, which might be why, when Kate's engagement to Prince William was announced, women across the world could be heard asking: Who's making the dress? What style will it be? How will it compare with Diana's? Charles and Diana's wedding on 29 July 1981 was watched by around 750 million people across the globe. William and Kate's April 2011 ceremony is expected to attract even more viewers, meaning that the pressure on Kate Middleton to choose the perfect wedding dress is immense. Royal protocol demands that her dress be suitably modest and demure (so no bare shoulders, thigh-skimming mini-frocks or use of colour for this bride). But she also has to cope with the fact that millions of people will be watching her wedding with the specific intention of judging her choice of dress, and then comparing it to that of her new husband's late mother, which, whether you loved or hated it, remains iconic in terms of bridal design. It's enough to have even the most resilient bride reaching for the smelling salts.

The Origin of the White Dress

In the Middle Ages, brides were expected to use their wedding dress and trousseau to show off their family's wealth and status, so it was not uncommon to see brides in bold colours and rich fabrics such as velvets, silks and even fur. The trend for white wedding dresses began in 1840, when Queen Victoria chose to marry in white, apparently because she'd taken a shine to Honiton lace and wanted to feature it on her dress. Prior to this, brides would marry in any colour, including black and blue, which was used to convey purity. White was reserved for christening gowns. The influence of Queen Victoria can also be felt in the style of dresses that many Western brides choose today. Up until the late 1930s, dresses tended to reflect contemporary fashion trends. Since then, there has been a move back towards Victorian styles, which usually feature long skirts, fitted or even corseted bodices, and veils.

Right: A portrait of Queen Victoria on her wedding day, 10 February 1840, and (far right) Elizabeth Bowes-Lyon, later to become the Queen Consort, pictured on the day of her marriage to Albert Duke of York on 26 April 1923.

Queen Victoria

Queen Victoria married Prince Albert on 10 February 1840, in the Chapel Royal of St James's Palace in London. A love match, the wedding brought with it a new tradition for British brides: that of the white wedding dress. Victoria's dress was made from pure white satin and Honiton lace. Her veil was also made from Honiton lace, with the total cost of lace estimated at £1,000 (about £72,100 in modern currency).

Elizabeth Bowes-Lyon, Queen Consort

When Elizabeth Bowes-Lyon, who was then a commoner (albeit one from noble stock), married Albert Duke of York at Westminster Abbey on 26 April 1923 she had no idea that, due to the abdication of her brother-in-law Edward VIII, she would one day become Queen Consort and later Queen Mother. Her wedding dress was designed by Madame Handley Seymour and was very much in keeping with the fashion of the period. This is reflected in the dropped waist, use of beading, and loose-fitting straight cut of the dress. Her wedding is probably more remarkable because the bride, who had lost a brother in the First World War, stopped to place her bouquet atop the Tomb of the Unknown Warrior on her way into the Abbey. This unexpected gesture has been copied by every royal bride since, though all have opted to dispense of their bouquets as they leave the Abbey, rather than when they enter it.

Queen Elizabeth II

The Queen was still Princess Elizabeth when she married Prince Philip on 20 November 1947 at Westminster Abbey. As Britain was recovering from the ravages of the Second World War, twenty-one-year-old Elizabeth was required to save up ration cards in order to buy the fabric for her Norman Hartnell gown, which was inspired by Botticelli's painting, *Primavera*, and featured 10,000 pearls, a fifteen-foot tulle train with white padded satin 'York' roses along the hem, and a cathedral-length veil.

Princess Margaret

Princess Margaret's wedding to photographer Antony Armstrong-Jones in Westminster Abbey on 6 May 1960 was the first royal wedding to be broadcast on television. Like her sister's, Margaret's dress was designed by Norman Hartnell. Groom Antony Armstrong-Jones was renowned for his eye for style, and suggested that Margaret's petite frame would be best suited to a classic unfussy design. The bodice had a v-neckline to elongate the bride's neck, and the waist was fitted to emphasise her slender figure. Like the bodice, the sleeves were also long and slim, giving the dress an air of simplicity. Her silk tulle veil was satin bound.

Princess Anne

At her Westminster Abbey wedding to her first husband Mark Phillips, which took place on 14 November 1973, Princess Anne wore a high-necked Tudor-style dress with medieval sleeves designed by little-known dressmaker Susan Small, and her mother's King George III Fringe Tiara. So radiant was she at the time that she even featured on the cover of *Vogue*. For her second wedding, to Timothy Laurence at Crathie Church near Balmoral Castle, on 12 December 1992, Anne chose a simple white, knee-length Nehru collared suit, and white blooms in her hair.

Clockwise from top left: Princess Elizabeth – later to become Queen Elizabeth II – and the Duke of Edinburgh on their wedding day, 20 November 1947; Princess Anne and her first husband Mark Phillips pose for a photograph after their wedding, 14 November 1973; Antony Armstrong-Jones and Princess Margaret wave to the assembled crowds from the balcony of Buckingham Palace on 6 May 1960.

Princess Diana

'This is the stuff of which fairytales are made,' opined the Archbishop of Canterbury as he presided over Charles and Diana's 1981 wedding service at St Paul's Cathedral, and many thought the same could be said of the bride's dress. Designed and made by British couturiers David and Elizabeth Emanuel under highly secretive conditions, the £500,000 silk taffeta dress not only included a v-necked pie-crust collar and enormous leg-of-mutton sleeves, it also contained over 100 metres of silk in the petticoat alone, not to mention a twenty-five-foot train. Often considered a mistake and indicative of the young Princess's lack of style savvy, the sheer volume of the dress – surely the one the term 'meringue' was coined for – combined with the unwise choice of fabric meant that by the time the young bride reached St Paul's it was visibly creased, something that was commented on around the globe.

❛Our first view of Diana, apart from in the morning when we put her through the carriage, was at the top of the steps, and you could see her head appearing first, then the skirt. "Oh my God! The creases!" I just nearly died in all honesty.❜

Elizabeth Emanuel

Princess Diana and Prince Charles leave St Paul's Cathedral in a gilded open-top carriage on their wedding day, 29 July 1981.

> ❛ I believe that she'll wear a tiara so I'd go for hair down with soft curls . . .with her effortless elegance and thick silky hair, the more natural she wears it, the better. ❜
>
> *Ian Carmichael, the Queen's hairdresser*

Sarah Ferguson

Sarah Ferguson married Prince Andrew in Westminster Abbey on 23 July 1986. For her wedding day, Ferguson had well-connected society dressmaker Lindka Cierach make an ivory duchesse satin dress worth an estimated £30,000. It featured a scooped neck, bugle beads on the bodice, padded shoulders and an enormous bow at the bustle that led into a seventeen-foot train. Cierach embroidered the train with the letter 'A' for Andrew, and an anchor and rose to represent the groom's military career. The bride's coat of arms also featured, as did bees and thistles.

Sophie Rhys-Jones

Sophie Rhys-Jones married Prince Edward at St George's Chapel in Windsor Castle on 19 June 1999. The bride wore a 'coat dress' by British designer Samantha Shaw. A relatively modern design, the gown was made from ivory silk organza and silk crepe, and had 325,000 crystals and pearls fastened along the neck, full-length sleeves and the train. Sophie also wore a silk tulle cathedral-length veil that had crystals scattered all over it, and a pair of Gina shoes with a three-inch heel which, like her dress, were made from ivory silk crepe.

Autumn Kelly

Though she doesn't hold the title of Princess, Montreal-born Autumn Kelly married the Queen's untitled eldest grandson Peter Phillips on 17 May 2008, at St George's Chapel in Windsor Castle. Made by designer Sassi Holford, the bride's decidedly modest £2,000 ivory silk dress was revealed to the public in a *Hello!* magazine feature on the wedding, for which the couple were reportedly paid £500,000.

Clockwise from top left: Sarah Ferguson and Prince Andrew walk arm-in-arm after their wedding ceremony on 23 July 1986; the Queen's eldest grandson Peter Phillips and his new bride Autumn Kelly walk hand-in-hand on their wedding day, 17 May 2008; Sophie Rhys-Jones and Prince Edward practice their 'royal wave' on well-wishers following their wedding at St George's Chapel in Windsor Castle, 19 June 1999.

The Diary of a Princess-in-Waiting:
How Kate Will Spend Her Wedding Day

Kate, who will be known as Catherine when she marries, can expect a long day. Her wedding, due to be held on a Friday, has been designated an official public holiday. With Easter falling the weekend before, and May Day holiday on the following Monday, many people will enjoy two four-day weekends in a row, meaning that there will be countrywide good will towards Kate and her husband-to-be. Pubs will also be permitted to extend their opening times until 1:00am so that the nation can celebrate.

7:00am: Catherine Middleton will have a choice of royal palaces at her disposal for the night before her wedding. Instead she may choose to spend her last night as a commoner at the Goring Hotel, which has already been hired to accommodate the royal wedding guests. The designer responsible for Kate's wedding dress will arrive early to help her prepare, along with a team of hairdressers and make-up artists who will be responsible for making the bridal party look suitably gorgeous, and allowing Kate to feel fully confident in front of the crowds, press and millions of people who will be watching her on television across the globe.

Perhaps most importantly, Kate's hairdresser will also be there in the morning (and probably throughout the day) to ensure her hair looks its swishy, glossy best. Sassi Holford, who made Autumn Kelly's dress, has said that this team of 'dressers' are likely to be permitted to wait outside Westminster Abbey – to get a good view of the wedding party leaving and entering – but will not be invited in.

10:00am: Kate will be taken to Westminster Abbey by car along a route that will include The Mall, Horse Guards Parade, Whitehall and Parliament Square – the route traditionally taken for the state opening of parliament. She is the first royal bride to have opted out of travelling in a horse and carriage since 1963. Previously, most have chosen the classic fairytale option so that the assembled crowds could get a good look at them. Modern-day Cinderella Kate may have chosen to travel by car for several reasons, including fears over security, her own inexperience of such large crowds, or her apparent desire to make her transformation from commoner to royal a true fairytale moment – it has been confirmed that when they leave the cathedral as

Queen Elizabeth II pictured with Princess Diana and four of her five bridesmaids – all of whom were under eighteen – on the day of her wedding to Prince Charles.

❝ I remember going to see Diana as she was getting ready in
her wedding dress and before that, she was just my big sister.
But then when I walked in that day, I thought, my goodness,
they've transformed her into, I have to say, a very beautiful woman.
She did become that day a sort of fairytale princess.
It was almost like she was handed over to the world that day. ❞

Charles, 9th Earl Spencer

a married couple, Kate and William will be transported back to Buckingham Palace by horse and carriage, so they can greet the assembled crowds.

11:00am: The wedding service will begin in front of a congregation of between 1,800 and 2,200 people, made up of the couple's family and friends, foreign dignitaries, and members of the public that Prince William has met through his charity work. According to an appalled *Daily Mail*, these may include 'drug addicts', as well as children and injured former servicemen. The bride's relatives will be on the left and the groom's on the right, with more senior guests arriving last and the Queen set to appear just before Kate.

Dr John Hall, the Dean of Westminster Abbey, will conduct the service itself, while Rowan Williams, the Archbishop of Canterbury, will marry the couple, leading them through their vows. Richard Chartres, the Anglican Bishop of London – who confirmed Prince William into the Church, and was a confidante of his mother – will then give a 'very personal' sermon.

1:30pm: The couple, now man and wife, will be taken to Buckingham Palace in a State Landau Coach (a rather impressive horse and carriage). The rest of the royal family will follow in procession. Thousands of marching soldiers, military bands and mounted regiments will also follow this route, creating an impressive spectacle ahead of the couple's wedding reception.

2:30pm: After spending some time having their official wedding photographs taken, the couple, along with the rest of the royal family, will take to the balcony of Buckingham Palace. The newlyweds' first kiss on the balcony is usually the part of the day the general public most look forward to.

At the same time, RAF pilots will stage a 'fly past' display in the skies over central London. While the photographs are being taken, the Queen will host a reception for guests from the wedding service who, according to Clarence House's Twitter feed, will represent 'the couple's official and private lives'. This state occasion will be a

> ❛ I just remember she had a cracking
> headache because she wasn't used to wearing a tiara. ❜
>
> *Earl Spencer, talking about his sister, Princess Diana, on her wedding day,*
> Entertainment Tonight, *May 2010*

Princess Diana and Prince Charles share their first public kiss as a married couple on 29 July 1981.

huge formal event and is expected to include a banquet of some sort, but will still only be open to less than half of the guests who attended the wedding ceremony.

For the first time, this reception will not include a formal wedding breakfast. Instead, guests will be served canapés and champagne before attending a buffet. It is usual for a dish to be specially created for this part of the day; at the Queen's wedding, dessert was Bombe Glacée Princess Elizabeth, a ball of ice-cream filled with mousse, custard, sorbet or another flavour of ice-cream, while Charles and Diana's guests filled up on a main course of Suprême de Volaille Princesse de Galles – chicken breasts stuffed with lamb mousse covered in brioche crumbs. There has been no confirmation of what non-traditionalist Kate and Wills will serve their guests, but it is hoped the reception will include 'something new'. Michelin-starred chef Michel Roux Jr, who serves on the royal wine-tasting committee, has suggested that a British vintage sparkling wine may be chosen to toast the royal couple, rather than the traditional champagne.

6I think she has got "it". But is the time right or the need for her to step into that mould? I've got a feeling not. With hindsight we saw why Diana spent rather a lot of time looking at herself. And I don't think that's going to be on the agenda for Kate. I think she's going into this with her eyes wide open. She's nearly ten years older than Diana was and she's clearly in a very loving relationship and I think it's quite, quite different. . .9

Bruce Oldfield

4:00pm: The newlyweds will be given some private 'downtime' to rest before the evening festivities begin. This is sure to be especially important for Kate, who is unused to royal occasions. (Princess Diana was apparently left with a splitting headache on her wedding day, because she wasn't used to wearing a tiara.)

7:00pm: William's father, the Prince of Wales, will give a private dinner followed by dancing for the couple, their close friends and family. This small, private function for between 250 and 300 guests will be much more relaxed and is expected to include champagne, cocktails and live music, much like wedding receptions up and down the country, but on a far grander scale.

The Honeymoon: Both Charles and Diana and the Queen and Prince Philip went straight to Broadlands in Hampshire to begin their honeymoon on the evening of their wedding days. Charles and Di then took an eleven-day cruise around the Mediterranean. William and Kate will spend their first night as man and wife at either Buckingham Palace or St James's Palace. They are expected to go on honeymoon the following day, Saturday, or on Sunday 1 May, and while the palace would not confirm where the newlyweds planned to head off to, it has been rumoured that the couple are likely to stay in the UK. The beautiful Isles of Scilly, just off the tip of Cornwall, are said to be top of the young couple's list.

It's certain that, wherever they end up, Kate will dress to impress

Kate arrives at the wedding of Sarah Louise Stourton and Harry Aubrey-Fletcher in January 2011, wearing a silk velvet coat by Libélula and a black pillbox hat by Whitely Fischer.

British Library Cataloguing in Publication Data
A catalogue record for this book is available from
the British Library

ISBN-13: 978-0-85965-476-0

Front Cover Photo by Mark Stewart/ Camera Press
Cover and book design by Coco Wake-Porter
Printed in Great Britain by Scotprint

Acknowledgements
I would like to thank Laura Coulman for getting me
involved in this project and for her editorial input,
and Laura Slater and Sandra Wake for their additional
research, which has proved invaluable. I would also
like to thank Tom Branton, who, along with Laura C,
provided editorial guidance and emails which, in the
spirit of *Kate Style*, we'll be calling 'classic, sophisticated
and good-humoured'. The input of Coco Wake-Porter,
who designed this book, cannot be overstated. I really
have appreciated the many hours of work she put into
getting the look of the book right. Thanks also to Marie
Chapman, who first suggested putting together a book
on Kate Middleton's dresses.
    Especially big personal thank yous to Craig
Fitzsimons, Alice and Alan Orme, my brother Alan
Healy Orme, Vance and Jackie Idiens, and my friends
Barbara Roterburg, Amanda Kavanagh, Paula Geraghty
and Laura Coulman for remaining friends with me
while I wrote this book, even though I didn't talk
about anything else for months. I won't forget your
encouragement and interest, so thank you. Special
mentions also to Kay, Kirsty and Billy Fitzsimons,
Eamonn James Farrell and Martin Newman, Josie, Brian,
Michelle and Shannon Maturi, Hunter, Murphy, Lefty
and Peppy Chavez.
    This book is dedicated to Vance Idiens, Edmund
Farrell and Niall O'Donnell, for entirely disparate
reasons.

The author and editors would like to thank the following
newspapers, magazines, websites, and television
programmes: Ticky Hedley-Dent at *The Daily Mail*, *The
Guardian*, *The Observer*, *Observer* magazine, *Observer
Woman*, *The Telegraph*, *The Times*, *The Sunday Times*,
Stella magazine, *Sunday Times Style* magazine, *The
Independent*, *The Irish Independent*, *The Financial Times*,
The New York Times, *New York* magazine, *Women's Wear
Daily*, *In Touch*, *The Metro*, *British Vogue*, *American Vogue*,
OK!, *Hello!*, *Heat*, *Closer*, *People* magazine, *Telegraph*
magazine, *GQ*, *USA Today*, *Star* magazine, *Vanity Fair*,
Tatler, *Grazia*, Vogue.co.uk, Harpersbazaar.com, Brides.
com, Hairdressers Journal Interactive, HowIlost20lbs.
com, Dailymail.co.uk, Telegraph.co.uk, CBSnews.com,
Style.com, RadarOnline.com, Stylist.com, Express.co.uk,
Windsorstar.com, BeautyEditor.ca, Elle.com, Jezebel.
com, Gawker.com, NadineJolie.com, *British Style Genius*
(BBC 2), *The Good Schools Guide*.
    We would also like to thank the following for
supplying photographs: Getty Images; Rex Features;
Camera Press; Tim Graham/ Getty Images; Indigo/
Getty Images; Anwar Hussein/ Getty Images; Anwar
Hussein/ WireImage; Stephen Lock/ Rex Features; Mark
Stewart/ Camera Press; Anwar Hussein/ Getty Images;
Tim Rooke/ Rex Features; Tim Graham/ Getty Images;
M Neilson/ Getty Images; Tim Graham/ Getty Images;
Steve Wood/ Rex Features; David Hartley/ Rex Features;
Claudia Bradby/ claudiabradby.com; Richard Young/ Rex
Features; Brendan Beirne/ Rex Features; Rotello/ Rex
Features; MCP; Ikon Pictures Ltd/ Rex Features; Alan
Davidson/ Rex Features; Davidson/ O'Neill/ Rex Features;
Stephen Butler/ Rex Features; Paul Webb/ Rex Features;
David Hartley/ Rupert Hartley/ Rex Features; Graham
Stone/ Rex Features; BIPNA/Keystone Collection; Danny
Martindale/ Getty Images; Tim Graham/ Getty Images;
Mark Stewart/ Camera Press; Tim Graham Royal Photos/
Getty Images; Ken McKay/ Rex Features; Chris Jackson/
Getty Images; Ben Stansall/ Getty Images; Hulton
Archive/ Getty Images; Mario Testino Handout/ Getty
Images; Vera Wang, Courtesy Photo/*Women's Wear Daily*;
Karl Lagerfeld, Courtesy Photo/*Women's Wear Daily*;
Badgley Mischka, Courtesy Photo/*Women's Wear Daily*;
Christian Lacroix, Courtesy Photo/ *Women's Wear Daily*;
Courtesy Photo/ *Grazia* issue 279 Dec. 2010; Courtesy
Photo/*OK! USA* issue 50 Dec. 2010; Valentino, Courtesy
Photo/ *Women's Wear Daily*; Ben de Lisi, Courtesy
Photo/ Hello! issue 1151 Nov. 2010; Michael Dunlea/ Rex
Features; c. Tavin/ Everett/ Rex Features; Hutton Archive/
Getty Images; Mark Large/ *Daily Mail*/ Rex Features;
Lichfield/ Lichfield Archive/ Getty Images; Michael
Dunlea/ Rex Features; Eddie Mulholland/ Rex Features;
Richard Heathcote/ Getty Images; Ikon Pictures Ltd/
Niraj Tanna/ Rex Features.